from Stewart Rowles Aug 93.

L. AYLSHAM.

On Stone by D. Hodgson, from a Drawing by Frances Stone & Son.

Printed by Engelmann Graf, Coindet & Cᵒ.

AYLSHAM LOCAL HISTORY SOCIETY

MILLGATE, Aylsham

A Study by
the Local History Research Group
edited by Tom Mollard

AYLSHAM
1993

ISBN 0 9521564 0 7

Catton Printing
13 Roundtree Close
Norwich NR7 8SX

Contents

Other publications of the Society

"Journal & Newsletter" (Quarterly) 1985 –

"Aylsham in the Seventeenth Century" 1988

"Aylsham in 1821" (Occasional Paper No.1) 1989

PREFACE

The chapters in this book are the work of several of the members of the research group whose names are recorded in the Chairman's foreword. Most chapters are the work of a single contributor pursuing one particular line of study, but others are the combined work of two or more people whose interests and researches overlapped.

Some of the original contributions contained more detail than has appeared in the final version of this book. Copies of the original contributions are now in the Parish Archives and may be consulted there.

The editor is grateful to each contributor, and particularly to Peter Holman who also provided the line drawings which illustrate the text.

Tom Mollard

Editor

Foreword

Soon after the Aylsham Local History Society was formed in 1984, Mr.Tom Bishop of Bridge House, Millgate, offered a bundle of deeds in his possession to the Society for examination, believing that they might be of historical interest. A quick superficial survey of their contents revealed that they indeed contained much information about properties mostly, but not entirely, in Millgate, and covered a period from about 1750 onwards. At this time, no one in the membership was available to study them in detail.

However, as the membership has grown, a 'research group' has come into being, and has been meeting regularly over a period of years, gradually acquiring some skills in reading and appraising documents.

Two years ago, the corner of Aylsham we call Millgate seemed a suitable portion of the town for group study. Mr.Bishop was happy to lend out his documents, and the project got under way with Christopher Barringer, Director of Extra-Mural Studies at the University of East Anglia, as tutor.

In our two years of study we have sought not only to learn what the "Bishop Bundles" (as they have come to be called) can tell us about Millgate, but to relate that information to that obtained from other historical sources. The resulting book is an account of what we have learnt about the properties in the area, the people who owned and lived in them, their life-style and how they earned their living during this period. Millgate emerges as an area of Aylsham made distinctive by its growth round the river and the mill, yet remaining an integral part of the larger market town community.

We are grateful to Christopher Barringer for his advice and support in the carrying forward of this project.

Contributors over the two year period include the following:-

Anne Applin, Ray Balls, Valerie Belton, Alan Coote, Eileen Daines, Julian Eve, Jill Fletcher, Elizabeth Gale, Geoffrey Gale, Betty Gee, Peter Holman, Tom Mollard, Kay Mosse, Jane Nolan, Frank Stageman, Maureen Strong, Joan Turville-Petre and Wenda Wiles.

Jane Nolan

Chairman
Aylsham Local History Society.

Chapter One

MILLGATE - An Introduction
by Christopher Barringer

The market town of Aylsham survives, relatively untouched by the processes of industrialisation in the nineteenth century and by the worst effects of the motor car, shopping malls, and the post-modern return to stockbrokers' Tudor that is fast afflicting housing estates. The beautiful parish church stands high above the valley of the River Bure with the market place close up against its southern side. The market place is surrounded by many sixteenth, seventeenth and eighteenth century buildings, as well as some more recent ones. Hungate, Red Lion and White Hart Streets lead to the market place and also have many fine pre-nineteenth century buildings bordering them. Two miles to the west of Aylsham lies the Blickling estate which provides a boundary to Aylsham on its western side, and has also had an important influence on the evolution and character of the town.

This book is primarily concerned with Millgate, the road which links the core of Aylsham around the market place with the water mill on the Bure. Millgate does, in some ways, qualify as the nineteenth century part of the town, although the important watermill almost certainly dates from pre-Domesday times, and a cluster of buildings between the mill and the 'great bridge' includes a number of pre-nineteenth century survivals. The opening of the Bure Navigation in 1779 linked Aylsham by canal and river with Yarmouth and the Broadland river system. The development led to the rapid growth of new occupations such as wherryman and boat builder, and also increased the outlets for the malting trade in Aylsham. This, in turn, led to families such as the Spurrells and Parmeters becoming important members of the Aylsham community. By focussing on a small part of the town, it was hoped that it would be possible to follow the fortunes of some families and some of their houses within a relatively limited part of the larger community of Aylsham.

This study does not aim to try to look at Millgate as far back as 1624, the date of an important survey of Aylsham which was transcribed and published as "Aylsham in the Seventeenth Century" [Aylsham 1988]. However, one or two points about the medieval organisation of Aylsham are important in understanding the sources that have been used.

The major manor of Aylsham was termed Aylsham Lancaster from about 1371, because it was part of the possessions of the Duchy of Lancaster, and Aylsham became the principal town of the Duchy in Norfolk. This was the largest of the Aylsham manors, and probably represents the bulk of the early pre-conquest unit or 'estate' that may have existed in late Saxon times. The northern part of the parish of Aylsham, in the main north of the Bure, formed a second manor that belonged, about 1200, to the Abbey of Bury St.Edmunds, and was presumably granted to Bury by the King out of his great manor. Some parts of this manor did reach across the river. After the Dissolution of the Monasteries in 1538 the Bury Manor was bought by Edward Wood, Mayor of Norwich in 1548, and the manor became known as that of Aylsham Wood. Finally, the vicarage of Aylsham also had a small manor attached to it, and its holdings were scattered through the town. The surviving records of the three manors of Aylsham Lancaster, Aylsham Wood and Aylsham Vicarage have all had to be consulted, as properties held of all the manors lay in Millgate, though the bulk of them were in the manor of Lancaster. The mill seems to have been within the main manor. Domesday (1086) refers to two mills, but the site of the second mill is not known with certainty.

Three other major sources have been used in reconstructing something of the more recent history of Millgate. The first was a large collection of deeds relating to those Millgate properties which has been collected by Mr.Tom Bishop. These have been a major quarry for this study. They are referred to throughout as the 'Bishop Bundles' and their contents are listed at the end of this work.

Secondly, the census returns for 1821, and 1841-81 have all been examined for Millgate, and provide a detailed inventory of all the people living in the street at the census day in each documented year. The census returns do not, however, tell us about those who left Millgate in the nineteenth century. We do not know, for example, if many families migrated to find work in the industrial towns of Midland and Northern England, or emigrated to Australia or the New World.

In addition, wills of the more prosperous members of the community up to 1857 have also been a valuable source, and help to throw light upon the details of at least some families. Sadly, inventories of household goods are of little help after about 1750.

One or two collections of family papers relate at least in part, to Millgate. Those of the Clover family have proved particularly interesting in revealing the business and family affairs of Joseph Clover, the portrait painter.

The records of Aylsham parish church are also of great value, but they have to be combed through in order to find items of particular relevance. Much has had to be discarded, interesting though it may be in other contexts.

Finally, there is the Aylsham town archive, housed in the Town Hall, which has a great deal of important material that has been accessible to the members of the group.

---ooOoo---

Millgate, near the Stonemason's Arms.

Chapter Two

MILLGATE - the scene today

Millgate, from the site of the old gasworks down to the river crossing, is a typical ancient way. It was the way to the mill as well as a leading out of the town to manorial fields, villages beyond, and eventually the coast.

As an ancient way it winds slightly, dropping gently downhill, and has many buildings standing on the edge of the roadway. There are no pavements, and the various frontages are staggered, often according to their age. The whole effect is of unplanned pleasantness and informality.

This effect has much to do with the use of local building materials. Clay for bricks and tiles was available locally. Other roofing materials were thatch of heather which grew - and still grows - on the open commons hereabouts, and reeds and sedge from the river marshes and the broads. Some of the older houses are timber-framed from local trees. Flint pebbles, brought from the beaches on the coast, were used in a very decorative way in the houses of the early nineteenth century when transport became easier. The use of pebbles of a regular size gives an unexpectedly pleasing effect, in contrast to the quoins of white-painted brick which make up the outline of the building. Numbers 3, 5, 7 and 9 are splendid examples of this style, with their sash windows set in a regular pattern, gable and chimney stacks and neat tiled roofs.

Numbers 3 and 5 are a pair, and sport an interesting centre panel based on a curving swastika design in flint. These early nineteenth century properties stand well back from the road with good front gardens, which enables one to get the full benefit of their trimness. Other properties using the same style and materials are Number 20 (on the east side) which uses small flint pebbles, and the row of cottages built by Mash, and dated W.E.M. 1845. These are three cottages with irregularly spaced windows, those on the ground floor having unusual cambered heads. They have small front gardens, but very long gardens run back to the rear. It is good to see that the old type of red telephone kiosk has been retained alongside them.

Numbers 3 & 5, Millgate.

In between these pebble-fronted dwellings there are colour-washed taller buildings which show signs of many alterations, but have value as a group. Below Number 20 is another recently altered property that was formerly the last shop in Millgate. A row of buildings stretching back from here, may have included some with some industrial uses.

Opposite these properties, at the top end of Millgate, is the island formed by New Road (an old part of Town Lane) and Bure Way (formerly Commercial Road, formerly Workhouse Lane). This contains a jumble of brick built properties, with Sycamore House, its datestone of 1815, looking firmly down the hill. New Road has some smallish houses, including Garner's Cottages dated 1869. There is also a solid Victorian Chapel built by the Methodists (Wesleyan Reform) which has passed through several denominations, and has recently been outgrown by the Tabernacle. Just below this is a flint-faced property which shows the scars of having been a butcher's shop. At the back of these premises was the site of the earliest workhouse in Aylsham.

Passing down this part of the street, the next prominent building is on the east side, and is the Stonemason's Arms, standing back a little with open parking space. Its stone quoins, string course and slate roof and regular frontage indicate a Victorian style for this solid-looking hostelry. It is the sole survivor of several other inns in Millgate. Below the Stonemason's Arms there is more Victorian building: a pair with the datestone - Victoria Place 1851 - with dormer windows, alongside some smaller properties of uncertain age.

Round the turning into Mill Row, there is a jumble of small, untidy gardens alongside a small tumbledown single cottage, much altered, pebble-dashed and with poor modern windows, but a building which still clings to some character.

Mill Row is a dead end leading to the watermill on the River Bure and to the Belt Farm. At one time several small cottages lined the beginning of the south side. Now there are gaps, and the ancient timber structures can be seen clinging to adjoining walls. There has also been some recent larger domestic building which leads to a contrast of old world charm and modern neatness. There is also infilling in the large garden of the Mill House. Nearer the Mill there is a long group of houses which form a pleasant secluded group in the presence of the bulk of the Mill itself, with the Mill House as the centre-piece with its solid brick indented quoins, probably dating from the eighteenth century. Although some of the other buildings show such alterations as filled-in archways and overlarge windows, the general effect is bearable within the group.

The Mill itself is an imposing building straddling the River Bure. When it stopped working, in 1967, it had two interior wheels which are still in place, along with some of the milling machinery. The facade facing the mill pond formed by the river dates from the late eighteenth century, and is the latest of the many mills that have stood on this site since before 1086, the time of the Domesday Book. With its three storeys, with about ten windows on each floor and white painted projecting locum (for hoisting sacks), and white doors, it reflects well in the still water in front of it, whereas on the lower side, the water dashes out into the pool where the wherries used to load and unload straight from the mill itself. Now the twentieth century has caught up with this fine building, as the rear portion has been neatly converted into holiday flats, whilst the main building houses a very large cinema organ! The relationship between the River Bure, the Mill and the navigation is complex, and can best be explained by a diagram-cum-map.

Returning to Millgate itself, there are interesting buildings on the west side, just above the entrance to Mill Row. Numbers 15 and 17 form an L-shaped block, with Number 15 gable end on the road, and showing a fine set of a dozen windows or so, and an off-centre door with a neat canopy. There are also the remains of a moulded brick string course. No.17 faces on to the road, and has an upper storey of roughly knapped flint, a simple door case, and a rough, squat stone cross on the north gable end.

The long building running back from the road is the Maltings, dated by a stone in the high gable end "Robert Parmeter 1771". Here, grain, mainly barley, was steeped, allowed to sprout, then roasted to produce malt for brewing. The building has recently been converted into dwellings. Note the original upstanding ridge tiles provided for ventilation. The other similar block standing back and parallel to the road, is modern though built of re-used bricks and tiles.

Stone House - looking down Millgate.

Opposite on the east side is Bure House. This imposing residence has a dated brick in its south wall incised with 'TR 1768' It is of three storeys with large sashed windows, a central door-way with a pedimented door case with Tuscan pilasters. There is a brick string course and fine eaves decoration. The rear of the building has a surprising number of blank window openings, and a long orchard-like garden running back towards the mill with a good coped brick boundary wall that forms the north side of Mill Row. Bure House also has a curious two and a half storey lean-to wing butting on to the road. From here down to the bridge over the river, the road used to be lined with small cottages crowding along the roadside, as can be seen in old postcards from early in this century. Only two or three small buildings now remain; one is a small antique business and another houses a church trust.

On the west side, before the bridge, stands Bridge House, formerly the Anchor Inn. This is a large building of considerable character with many interesting details which include a fine door case and fanlight, good sashed windows, and three large dormer

9

windows in a pantiled roof. The north end, overlooking the river, is a large shaped gable in the Flemish style, built to impress when approached from the north.

Why the river crossing is situated here is not obvious, but here stood the 'great brygge over the Kings river at Aylesham. . . . which brigge is a common passage for horse and carte both to the market at Aylsham and to the coaste for the countrie'. This wooden structure was the responsibility of the parish. In 1547 church plate was disposed of, partly to cover repairs to the bridge, and also to avoid the parish losing the value of the plate. In 1759 the great bridge was replaced by the present brick structure, and bears the date and name of the builder - W.Berry. This simple single arch has withstood several severe floods. The next, equally narrow, brick bridge was built in 1821, and is over the feeder to the Navigation, which also acts as a relief channel to the Mill.

Beyond this feeder channel stands Nos. 1 & 2 Mash's Row of 1845, facing the road, with red brick dressings containing a pebble flint frontage, and said to have been built as yet another inn. Nos. 3-6 follow on round the corner at right angles.

Here Millgate merges into Drabblegate. The layout of the roads has changed several times since the arrival of the Navigation in 1779, the railway in 1880 and finally the by-pass in 1980. Dunkirk, and what was the lane leading to Tuttington, are now lined by modern mills and silos, industrial buildings, and estates sufficiently separated from the older charms and informality of Millgate itself, to cause no clash between the old and the new.

---ooOoo---

Chapter Three

THE NAVIGATION AND THE STAITHE

The idea of making use of the River Bure (or the North River, as it was sometimes called) goes back a long way in the history of Aylsham. Sapwell, in his history of the town, quotes from the churchwardens' accounts of 1708-10 the expenditure of the considerable sum of £13-9-4 for "viewing and measuring the river to make it navigable". The river is tidal up to Coltishall, and even earlier, the Romans had exported large quantities of pottery from Brampton, by water, down to the coast.

It would seem that the idea of speculating in making the river navigable drew several of the local landed gentry together to obtain an Act of Parliament for the construction of five locks and the digging of new channels to cut off sharp bends. The Act was obtained in August 1773 at a cost of £304-3-2. The Commissioners sworn in included the names of Walpole, Buckingham, Thos.Durrant, A.Marsham, Thos.Robins, Jno.Smith, J.Gay, James Curtiss and a Mr.Pepper - a miller at Buxton. They expected the cost of construction to be about £6,000, and from somewhere an engineer by the name of H.A.Biodermann, who had produced an excellent plan of the scheme, dated 1772, appeared, and took over the laying out of the "land to be staked out". Samuel Robinson, a contractor, undertook to do most of the work for £4,200, but failed to turn up to direct the work, and Biodermann was appointed to take charge. The early accounts are very detailed, and payments show that the money was running out as the considerable alterations to the course of the river at Burgh were undertaken by local builders and gangs of workmen paid by Biodermann. It would seem that this was as big an engineering undertaking as this part of rural Norfolk had ever seen before.

The Commissioners met alternately at the Black Boys in Aylsham market place and The Dog Inn, which stood at the top of the Norwich

Road, and dealt as best they could with the need for more and more money. In 1778, a new contractor was found to finish the constructional work. John Smith signed the agreement with a flourish on the map of the canal alongside many of the signatures of the Commissioners. However, by August of 1779, John Smith had decamped, leaving the work unfinished, and advertisements placed by the Commissioners in newspapers in London and York failed to locate him.

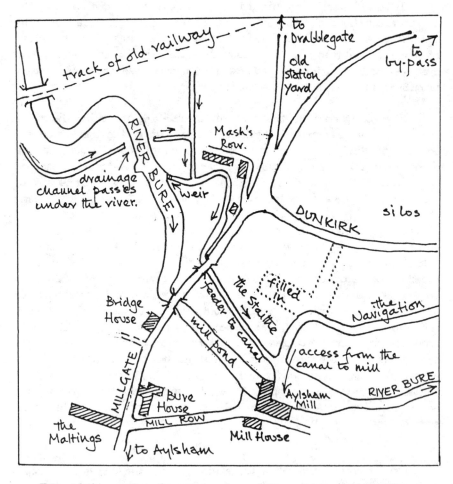

Diagram map of waterways and present road pattern at Millgate.

The Navigation was completed to the Staithe at Aylsham in late 1779, and brought prosperity to Millgate and Aylsham. At a time of bad local roads, the ability to transport heavy loads quickly and cheaply was a great asset. Wherries had traded on the Broads, where every village had a parish staithe. Loads could be taken down to Yarmouth, and transhipped for the coastal trade. The Navigation connected Aylsham to the Broads, and was designed to be used by the wherries under sail. The wherries were of 16 tons burden and drew $3\frac{1}{2}$ feet of water. There was no tow path, and locks were broader than on other waterways. Until recently, there were some who could remember seeing the great sails gliding quietly through the countryside.

Aylsham Staithe became a busy place, and expanded greatly from Biodermann's original oval "Key" (as marked on his map) which was built on land owned by Edmund Jewell. Extra basins were added and warehouses built. As well as the transport of goods in and out, there was the repair and building of wherries. Those who worked at the Staithe lived in Millgate, and families of wherrymen resided there over many generations. There was also work to be done on the maintenance of the canal, which tended to silt up. Constant 'didling' (dredging) and weed cutting had to be done, and bridges and locks suffered from damage.

The goods transported varied greatly - some now seem strange and unknown - and from the toll books the following have been noted:-

Barley	Coals	Fish salt	Flour
Pollard	Billet*	Maize	Seed
Beans	Gravel	Manure	Malt
Osiers	Hay	Wheat	Cinders
Deal timber	Scales(Meal?)		Cake
Marl	Wool.		

(*small twigs and bark for curing fish)

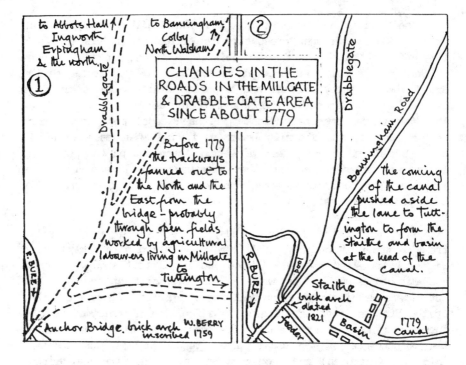

Map ①:

to Abbots Hall
Ingworth
Erpingham
& the north.

Drabblegate

① CHANGES IN THE ROADS IN THE MILLGATE & DRABBLEGATE AREA SINCE ABOUT 1779

Before 1779 the trackways fanned out to the North and the East from the bridge – probably through open fields worked by agricultural labourers living in Millgate to Tuttington

R. BURE

Anchor Bridge. brick arch inscribed 1759 W. BERRY

Map ②:

to Banningham, Colby North Walsham

②

Drabblegate

Banningham Road

the coming of the canal pushed aside the lane to Tutt-ington to form the Staithe and basin at the head of the canal.

R. BURE

Staithe brick arch dated 1821

Feeder

Basin

1779 canal

Passengers were taken down to Yarmouth and back. It must have been a pleasant way to travel compared with the jolting journey by road. The Navigation never made great profits for its promoters, probably because the initial expenditure had been so high. Tolls taken between 1780 to 1790 were, for example:-

	£		£		£
1780	177	1784	222	1788	265
1781	275	1785	169	1789	208
1782	316	1786	278	1790	215
1783	278	1787	259		

Under the original Act of Parliament manure and marl were not charged tolls, but the wherrymen had to be watched - on 3rd.April 1780 one Jarvis was fined £5 for giving a false account of his lading. Many of the cargoes were connected with milling and with local crops. Although the owners of the five mills along

14

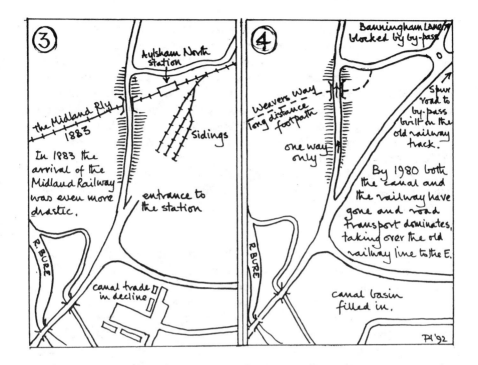

③ Aylsham North station

the Midland Rly 1883

In 1883 the arrival of the Midland Railway was even more drastic.

R. BURE

Sidings

entrance to the station

canal trade in decline

④ Banningham Lane blocked by by-pass

Weavers Way long distance footpath

one way only

Spur road to by-pass built on the old railway track.

By 1980 both the canal and the railway have gone and road transport dominates, taking over the old railway line to the E.

R. BURE

canal basin filled in.

PL '92

the river (Horstead, Buxton, Oxnead, Burgh and Aylsham) all objected originally to the making of the Navigation, on the whole they eventually benefitted, using their own wherries to transport goods to and from their mills. There were disputes about the use of water for turning their mill wheels, and the use of water to fill the various locks, which were nearly all at mill sites. Marker stones were set in the river bank to determine the water levels.

However, the Navigation did benefit the area through which it ran, transporting materials for agriculture - manure, lime, marl - as well as for local industries. Frederick Starling, a basket maker, remembered in 1860 agents from the great Yorkshire wood firms, going round the neighbouring estates to buy up very large oak trees for shipbuilding. Gangs of Yorkshire working men lodged with cottage people in Millgate, whilst they cut up the timber and loaded it on to wherries to be taken down to Yarmouth for shipment to the north of England.

At the beginning of this century, wherrymen were paid by the voyage. The headman or captain got 35/- for a round trip from Aylsham to Yarmouth (40 miles) and back. He had to find a capable hand to work under him. The voyage took, on average, a week, with fair winds (which came free!), but three return voyages might be made in a fortnight. At that time, an average of three wherries left Aylsham every week, but by that time the canal trade had been hit by the railways which had arrived in the 1880s. The goods yard of the Midland Railway was within a stone's throw of the canal staithe - probably put there on purpose. By 1904, the annual tolls had declined from £404 in 1893 to £278, and the canal owners were trying hard to reduce their costs whilst maintaining a useable waterway.

The useable end came in 1912, when an immense flood swept down the Bure valley, washing away weirs and locks, altering the channel of the river, and destroying and damaging the bridges. The Commissioners had no money to re-instate the Navigation, and had no response to their appeals for help to various government bodies. The Great War hindered any recovery, and the disposal of the remains lingered on until 1928 when the County Council finally, and reluctantly, agreed to the transfer of the little remaining property into its care.

Nowadays, the locks have been adapted to control the flow of the water down the river; much of the Staithe at Aylsham has been filled in, though some old buildings remain standing, and the River Bure still flows placidly on, perhaps pondering on man's attempt to make use of its clear waters.

---ooOoo---

Chapter Four

AN INTRODUCTION TO THE PEOPLE OF MILLGATE

The people who appear in the next three chapters lived at a time when farming, and the trades and services associated with it, were relatively profitable. Yeomen farmers and grocers, millers and millwrights, a barber surgeon and a tanner were all able to afford copyhold land in Millgate, over and above what they had elsewhere. The eighteenth century saw many improvements in agriculture, and the outbreak of war with France in 1793 ushered in a period of even greater prosperity for farming. Although there was widespread rural unrest after 1815, prosperity returned in the 1830s, and continued until the 1870s. It is against this background that our families should be seen.

Each represents distinctive elements in the economic and social make-up of Millgate. Many who lived in Aylsham in the eighteenth century bought copyhold land in Millgate; James Curties is an example. He belonged to a well-established family of grocers who had been in that business for nearly a century. After his death in 1801, much of his land passed, indirectly, to John Fielde, a millwright, who accumulated a sizeable estate in Millgate by 1837. Another millwright, Thomas Harvey, also had land, and through his wife Ann, was connected with the foundation of the first Baptist Church in Aylsham.

Millgate attracted not only the inhabitants of Aylsham, but also people from neighbouring villages. John Power had been a farmer in Alby, before he became a barber surgeon in the town, and John Wickes, father of William Wickes who bought the Belt Estate in Millgate, was a tanner from Blickling. John Fielde came from Saxthorpe.

The Mill itself was naturally the commercial hub of the area. After the opening to navigation of the River Bure between Coltishall and Aylsham in 1779, and the development of staithes, warehouses and boatyards, new opportunities for profit and employment presented themselves. Thomas Spurrell, miller and maltster, farmed land. The Parmeters who succeeded him, did so too, but were also merchants and took an active part in the public life of Aylsham. William Mash continued the family tradition of farming, but combined it with being landlord of the Anchor Inn, and pursuing the building trade. Three generations of the Wright family were boatbuilders or watermen.

Whilst farming and milling remained lucrative occupations during the period, the story of these families shows a diversity of employment in the prosperous district of Millgate. This diversity is reflected in the types of houses which appeared in the area, ranging from the large homes of the prosperous traders and landowners to the humbler cottages of the people they employed.

Over the period we are exploring, many hundreds of people lived or worked, or owned property in Millgate. Of the majority of these people, we know nothing. In some instances we may know their names, but in most cases we do not even know that. These are the people that Ketton-Cremer describes so vividly in the introduction to one of his books,

'As for the mass of the population, the workers in the fields, the wrights and smiths in the villages, the weavers and dyers and fullers in the towns. . .they have left little memorial of their lives and their toil. "They took their wages and are dead"; and seldom, outside the pages of parish registers and parish accounts can even their names be recovered.'

Without knowing their names, we can still know something of what they did and how they lived, their occupations and their recreations.

18

In the first of the next three chapters we will look at the watermill and some of the millers and millwrights associated with it, but in the second chapter "People and Trades" we can explore this aspect from studies of the directories and of the census returns that cover the period, and we can obtain a picture of some of the unknown people of Millgate. In the succeeding chapter "Some Millgate Families," we can look in greater detail at some of that minority of people who were more fully recorded; those people, who for one reason or another, left some mark of their passing. These are the people who are recorded in legal documents as owners of properties, partners in sales, inheritors of land, or simply through their profession, left a record that brings their lives up to the surface from out of the mass of the unknown.

Chapter Five

AYLSHAM MILL AND SOME OF ITS MILLERS

It seems certain that a watermill has been in existence for many centuries near the spot where Millgate crosses the river Bure; possibly since Saxon times. There are two mills recorded in Domesday, the other probably being the mill at Bolwick.

About 1190, the Millgate mill was granted to the Abbot of St.Edmundsbury, as part of Sexton's Manor, but by 1370 it had reverted to the Crown, and was let to a series of tenants. Its history remains fairly obscure until the 17th.century, when the mill featured in a series of lawsuits, and through the records of these disputes the names of some of the owners or tenants emerge. In 1648 the mill was let to Captain Doughty for £60 per annum. A Tithe court held at the Black Boys on 13th.June 1682, "elicited some evidence as to the rights of the Vicar to tithes from the mill". It also throws up some names - Richard Bloome, miller, stated that he had known the mills for over fifty years, and had heard that John Neave had farmed them at a rent of £100 a year, and that Mark Throry farmed them at £70 or £80. All the defendants in the suit had been successive occupiers of the mills, and whilst they had been there, "the mills were well wrought, and did grind great quantities of corn and grain".

For those few years the occupiers of the mills had been:-

William Purdy	1670-71
William Throry	for about a year
Bartholomew Wilkes	1675-78
Robert Sexton	until 1680
Miles Baispoole	in 1683 gave Robert Doughty £3,750 for the mill and its lands.

This Robert Doughty was the son of an earlier Robert Doughty who had held the mill for 20 years before settling it on his son in 1673 on his marriage. William Smyth was a tenant from 1696-99, and in his time the mills were ruinous, and out of repair and required an outlay of £100 to make them tenantable.

THOMAS SPURRELL

Our knowledge of individual millers in the 18th.century starts with Thomas Spurrell, who is described in documents as a miller in Aylsham as early as 1743. He had considerable properties in and around the town, and is buried in the central aisle of the nave in St.Michael's church.

Thomas Spurrell seems to have had no family apart from a brother, who was a baker in Norwich, and a number of nephews and nieces. In his will of 1771 he expressed the wish that, "all those my watermills, called Aylsham mills and their appurtenances" and all his other properties (not itemised) should be sold, and the proceeds and his personal effects shared amongst these relatives and his housekeeper, Mary Hammond. She and Thomas Harvey, a millwright, of Aylsham and Joseph Ames, miller at Hellesdon, were his executors. His final wish was:-

"On the day of my burial, the bells may ring in the manner as they did for the burial of Mr.Edmund Jewell recently, and that the Aylsham ringers ring the Bumbled peal".

According to the Shorter Oxford Dictionary, this does not mean a muffled peal, as one might expect, but a booming note - "a loud, deep resonant sound".

THE PARMETER FAMILY - Robert the Elder, William, Robert the Younger and Samuel. [see family tree]

The death of Thomas Spurrell coincided with the coming of the Canal Age and a new era for Millgate. The Aylsham Navigation Act

22

was passed in 1773. Some of the key figures now emerging on the Millgate scene are those of Robert Parmeter and his children and grandchildren. Just exactly when the Parmeter family came to own the Aylsham mill is not clear, but by 1763 Robert was paying the Poor Rate for Aylsham mill. When Thomas Spurrell died in 1771, Robert Parmeter bought some of his copyhold properties, including what was later to become the Anchor Inn, and may well also have acquired the mill at this time.

In 1771, Robert Parmeter built the maltings, and around this time he also invested money [£220] in the Navigation "advanced on the credit of the tolls". From this time onwards the Parmeters steadily acquired property, mostly in and around the Millgate area, but also in Hungate Street and elsewhere in Aylsham. There are regular entries in the Manor Court Books of Aylsham Wood and Lancaster from this time until well into the nineteenth century, although these are not always readily identifiable.

Robert the Elder died in 1791 leaving his Hungate Street property to his unmarried daughter, Christian, and the Anchor Inn to his married daughter, Anne Lungley. The rest went to his second son, William, who sadly died two years later, of consumption, leaving his recent inheritance to his brother, Robert. Robert was the miller at Ingworth, and it seems that he took over the Aylsham mill, but may have continued to live at Ingworth for some time, as his older children were baptised in Ingworth church. His brothers, George and John, became millers in Ingworth and Burgh respectively. William's will shows the extent of the property he inherited from his father:-

"I give and devise all that my messuage and dwellinghouse wherein I now dwell, together with the malthouses, granaries, houses outhouses, yards, gardens, orchards, lands and grounds. . . being in Millgate Street in Aylsham. . .to Robert Parmeter, my brother. Also, subject as aforesaid, I give all that my estate and interest and terms of years yet to come and unexpired, of and in, all that staithe, yard, grounds and bank with the

23

THREE GENERATIONS OF PARMETER MILLERS

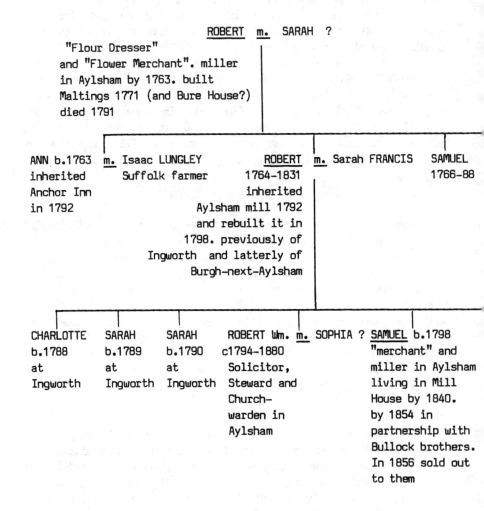

ROBERT m. SARAH ?

"Flour Dresser"
and "Flower Merchant". miller
in Aylsham by 1763. built
Maltings 1771 (and Bure House?)
died 1791

| ANN b.1763
inherited
Anchor Inn
in 1792 | m. Isaac LUNGLEY
Suffolk farmer | ROBERT
1764-1831
inherited
Aylsham mill 1792
and rebuilt it in
1798. previously of
Ingworth and latterly of
Burgh-next-Aylsham | m. Sarah FRANCIS | SAMUEL
1766-88 |

| CHARLOTTE
b.1788
at
Ingworth | SARAH
b.1789
at
Ingworth | SARAH
b.1790
at
Ingworth | ROBERT Wm. m. SOPHIA ?
c1794-1880
Solicitor,
Steward and
Church-
warden in
Aylsham | SAMUEL b.1798
"merchant" and
miller in Aylsham
living in Mill
House by 1840.
by 1854 in
partnership with
Bullock brothers.
In 1856 sold out
to them |

24

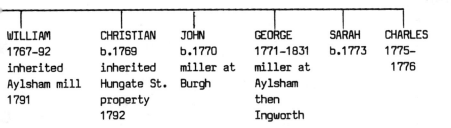

WILLIAM	CHRISTIAN	JOHN	GEORGE	SARAH	CHARLES
1767-92	b.1769	b.1770	1771-1831	b.1773	1775-
inherited	inherited	miller at	miller at		1776
Aylsham mill	Hungate St.	Burgh	Aylsham		
1791	property		then		
	1792		Ingworth		

FRANCIS b.1799
"Merchant and beer
brewer" of Booton.
Owned 'Bull Inn'
with William
Bircham

Rev.JOHN DENT
of Alderford
b.1801

warehouses, houses and buildings erected in part of the same situate, standing, lying and being next Aylsham Navigation, and also all those my subscriptions or shares of £220 lent and advanced on the credit of the tolls of the said Navigation, by the said Robert Parmeter, my father, deceased, and all interest to my brother, Robert."

Robert's inheritance was made conditional on his allowing their mother, Sarah, to continue to live in their house "in whatever rooms she chooses". He also left £100 to each of his brothers and sisters.

The Maltings, from Mill Row.

Robert the Younger seems to have been able, shrewd and energetic. He was described by Arthur Young, on his travels, as "a good farmer, and a very intelligible man". He acquired further property near Aylsham river in 1795, and a year later, the extensive Millhouse properties on Mill Row, which Thomas Harvey, the millwright and executor of Thomas Spurrell's will, had taken up in 1771. This was in the form of three adjoining messuages or dwelling houses, at one time the home of Thomas Spurrell and his housekeeper, Mary Hammond, then of Thomas Harvey, and now the home of Sarah Parmeter, with barns, stables, carthouses and other buildings, yards and gardens, containing in all, two acres. Later, these are described as the Millhouse, with a cottage on the west, and a counting house on the east. There were also more distant portions of meadow land, near the Aylsham to Tuttington Road.

In 1798, the mill was rebuilt in its present form. In 1804, he bought a further two acres of land between the Navigation and the river, and two years later, land which seems to abut on to the present Bure House property - possibly the 'double cottages' of later documents.

He married Sarah Francis, a member of a well-known Aylsham family. They had four children: Robert William, Samuel, Francis and the Rev. John Dent. Of these, it was Samuel who became the next generation miller. It is not known whether, as a family, Robert and Sarah lived in one of the family houses (Bure House and the Mill House) and, if so, for how long. At some stage they moved to Burgh-next-Aylsham, and he and Sarah are buried in Burgh church.

Samuel's older brother, Robert William, became a solicitor, and he and his wife, Sophia, seem to have contributed much to the life of the town and the church. They lived in the house, now called Parmeters, in Cromer Road, and are remembered in the church by a plaque in the wall of the choir, and the gift of "a warming apparatus" for use in inclement weather, given by their daughter, about 1880.

Although the Parmeter family held the mills for many years, from roughly 1771 to the middle of the 19th.century, the mills were actually advertised for sale by auction in 1795. Ownership clearly never left the Parmeter family, but the auction notice in the Norfolk Chronicle for 26th.September 1795 gives a useful picture of the extent of the property concerned:-

> To be sold by auction by Robert Ansell, at the Black Boys in Aylsham on Tuesday 6th.October next at 3 o'clock in the afternoon. . .the following estates in Lots.

Lot 1. All those large and valuable water corn mills called Aylsham mills, with two water wheels, one with counter motion, the other Spurr; with four pair of French stones, four flour mills, two rolling screens together with all the going gears, irons, brasses and appurtenances belonging to the said mills, also three stables, granary, barn, waggon lodge and other convenient buildings near the mills, in very good repair; with gardens and pightle adjoining, containing about 2 acres.

A very good and convenient messuage, pleasantly situated near the mills, and fronting the river with gardens adjoining now in the use of Mrs Parmeter.

Also a new-built dwelling house adjoining the last, in the occupation of Mr.William Cook.

And a very good cottage near the mills, very convenient for a servant of the miller to live in.

These mills are now in the occupation of Mr.Parmeter, without lease; are well situate for trade, being at the head of the Navigation. . . etc.

Lot 2. A Close of very good arable land, next the highway leading from Aylsham to North Walsham containing about 5 acres.

Lot 3. A Close of arable land containing about 2a; 2r; next the Kings Highway leading from Aylsham to Tuttington.

Lot 4. A Close of meadow or pasture, called the Furze meadow, next
the said road leading to Tuttington, containing about
5a; 1r; 34p; more or less.

Lot 5. A Close of very good meadow land, called Bears meadow,
containing about 4a; 2r; 16p; next the said road leading
to Tuttington.

Lot 6. Another meadow adjoining the last, containing about
3a; 2r; 33p;

All the above lands are lying in Aylsham aforesaid, at a short
distance from the mills, and now in the use of the said Mr.Parmeter
without lease.

Lot 7. A very good staithe, near the head of the Navigation, 75ft.
long with a large warehouse lately built upon it, brick and
tiled with double floor, very convenient for a merchant.

THE BULLOCK BROTHERS

Samuel Parmeter, in White's Directory of 1845, is described
as Corn miller and maltster, and proprietor of a wherry service
to Yarmouth along with Messrs. Copeman and Soame. He seems to have
had no children, and went into partnership with John Thornton Bullock
and his brother Stanley, finally selling out to them in 1856. They
bought, and almost immediately mortgaged for £5000 (with interest
at 5% per annum), the freehold property of the Watermills, Mill
Dam and Mill Pool, Dam Meadow, the Maltings and some other land,
and the extensive copyhold properties including the Millhouse and
cottages and counting house, Bure House and the double cottages
to the north. Later on, they were allowed a further £2000 mortgage
on the properties.

By 1889 they were heavily in debt, apparently due to John
Thornton Bullock's inefficiencies. William Foster, the Aylsham
solicitor, became trustee of all the Bullock properties and
responsible for paying off debts, while Stanley Bullock became

manager of the business. An indenture of 1893 tells us that debts had been paid off, without sale or surrender of properties. These properties, both freehold and copyhold, were conveyed to Stanley Bullock.

Both brothers were dead by 1914, and the mill was bought by Barclay, Pallett & Co. who already owned the Dunkirk Roller Mills which they had bought in 1907 on the retirement of Ben Cook.

For the subsequent history of the mills, see Ben Rust's article in the Journal of the Aylsham Local History Society. Volume 3, Number 6; June 1992.

---ooOoo---

Chapter Six

PEOPLE AND TRADES

The Millgate community, essentially a part of Aylsham, was divided from the town by a large area of open ground below White Hart Street, and this dividing swathe of countryside was continued eastwards by the Belt Estate. The links between Millgate and the rest of Aylsham were by two roads; Town Lane, a turning off White Hart Street, and Gay's Lane (later renamed as Gas House Hill), and a continuation of White Hart Street.

In the nineteenth century, although Town Lane was a narrow street, it appears to have been the more important of these two roads. However, road widening in this century has reversed their status, and today it is a narrow one-way lane. These two roads eventually meet at the start of Millgate, just below the site where the gas works was eventually established in 1850.

We can learn much about the people of Millgate and their everyday life from the directories and census returns of the period. In 1821, 370 people lived in Millgate. This was a fifth of the population of Aylsham. As Aylsham expanded, Millgate remained much the same size for lack of space, and it housed a smaller percentage of the town's population, as the following figures show:-

Year	Pop. of Aylsham	Pop.of Millgate	%
1821	1,853	370	20%
1851	2,741	352	12%
1871	2,505	339	14%
1881	2,674	410	15%

By the mid 19th.century, Millgate had three public houses: The Anchor Inn, near the bridge, The White Horse, halfway up the hill, and the Stonemason's Arms opposite. John Freeman, who kept the Stonemason's Arms, was a stonemason and at one stage employed four men and two apprentices in his yard beside the pub.

31

The river and the Navigation created considerable employment. The water power was harnessed to drive the two wheels of the large mill, which in 1851 was providing employment for 19 men. The watermill and the Navigation are described separately in Chapters 3 & 5, but it is worth repeating here what major sources of employment they were to Millgate and its people. In 1830 Robert Parmeter operated a regular wherry service from Millgate to Yarmouth. In 1845 the weekly service was shared between Samuel Parmeter, Copeman & Soames, corn and coal merchants in Dunkirk, and Thomas Shreeve, Corn, Cake and General Merchant, from the staithe at Millgate. It had developed by 1850 into a daily service and continued as such until the end of the century when once again it reverted to a weekly service, probably because of the competition from the railways.

Secondary trades also were created. The river wherries were the principal means of transport between Aylsham and the coastal ports, and consequently much of this secondary work was directly associated with the river trade. An average of 15 men were employed on the waterfront, but carters, hauliers, a wheelwright, harnessmaker and blacksmith were all closely associated with the waterways. Work on the waterfront continued in importance even after the arrival of the railways in 1880. It was the great floods of 1912 which destroyed all this when wherries were no longer able to reach Aylsham. Boat building and a boat repair yard had been established on the east side of the canal. This business which was run by different generations of the Wright family and employed several workers, was lost at the same time.

One of the largest employers in Millgate was Robert Bartram, described as a master builder and farmer. He was also a stone and marble mason who also dealt in Staffordshire tiles. His father, William, also a builder, had been a carpenter, timber merchant and coal dealer. At one time the firm employed 26 men, ten of whom lived in Millgate.

However, agriculture always remained the largest source of employment throughout this period. One can understand this; fields and meadows reached almost into Millgate, and census returns show how closely Millgate people were connected to the land:-

Principal occupations of Male workers in Millgate

Year	Agricultural	Watermen	Building	Milling
1821	39	-	-	-
1851	51	7	11	8
1861	41	15	8	7
1871	36	12	6	4
1881	40	17	16	5

A basket maker employed five men, and in 1851 had two apprentices. Women were employed as servants, dressmakers, straw bonnet makers, cooks, shop hands, a laundress, milkwomen and a schoolmistress.

This part of Aylsham also housed the Workhouse, which served the whole parish. This was built in 1776 on part of the land left by Thomas Cressy "for the use of the poor people of. . . Aylsham" This Thomas Cressy was, in fact, the uncle of the Thomas Cressy mentioned in Sapwell as churchwarden in 1638. The charity he founded still exists today and the details of it are set out in his will of 1613 written two years before his death:-

'I doe give and devise unto Simon Smith, Robert Doughtie and John Barker of Ailsham aforesaid evermore All those my houses and tenements situate and beinge in Ailsham aforesaid in a street called Millgate Domicilia Called or known by the name of or names of Smith and Grickes contayning twelve small dwellings. . . for the use of the poore people of the said town of Ailsham'

The will goes on to ensure the financing of this project by arranging for the rents and profits of lands and grounds adjoining these properties for repair and maintenance 'of the said houses forever'. He further directs that the 'overplus of the profitts' of the said lands and grounds which remain shall yearly be distributed to the said poor of Aylsham at the discretion of the churchwardens. When one of the trustees dies, 'the other two surviving are to choose another inhabitant of the said town to join with them in his stead and soe to continue from age to age forever.'

He reiterates that 'the said twelve severall dwellings shall be from time to time maintained forever without sufferinge anie of them to be lett down or impayred'

When the workhouse was built later, it was capable of housing 100 inmates, but it usually held only a third of that number. Two cottages remaining were let and the income used to support the workhouse. In 1836 the Aylsham Union was formed, and in 1837 the Aylsham workhouse was abandoned. The new Union workhouse was built in Cawston Road in 1849 to serve all 46 villages in the Union. This building is now St.Michael's Hospital. During the period between the closure of the parish workhouse and the opening of the Union workhouse, the Aylsham needy were housed at Cawston and Buxton.

The parish workhouse building was still standing after its abandonment long enough to be recorded in the 1839 Wright's map, [schedule No.298] so that we do know its precise location. It was demolished in 1842, and the land sold in 1856. The income from the investment of the proceeds is still distributed today as part of the combined parish charities.

By studying the census returns we can discover how many of the inhabitants of Millgate were natives of the town. More women came from outside the area than did men. Perhaps the men looked for a wife in the neighbouring villages. The 1871 census, used as an example, reveals the following pattern:-

Place of birth	Male	Female
Aylsham	118	88
Adjacent parishes	2	21
Other parts of Norfolk	27	51
Norwich	6	5
Other counties	13	8
TOTALS	166	173

The few shops in Millgate were mixed businesses. The baker sold groceries, the stonemason was also the landlord of the Stonemason's Arms. Fish was cured and sold by the landlord of the Anchor Inn, who probably kept his fish in the fishponds at the rear of the inn, and the landlord of the White Horse was also the butcher, a slaughterer and a farmer.

Today, all the shops have vanished. Some have become houses, but their conversions betray their previous use, and the shape of the shop windows can still be detected. The watermill no longer functions as a mill, the butcher's shop and the timber yard have vanished and the gas works have closed. The Millgate Nurseries which were established in 1929 are replaced by houses and bungalows in Stuart Close, the Anchor Inn and the White Horse are now private houses. Today, the Stonemason's Arms is the last surviving inn in Millgate.

---ooOoo---

Chapter Seven

SOME MILLGATE FAMILIES

After looking at the people of Millgate in general, we can now turn to some specific personalities or families who were part of the Millgate scene.

JAMES CURTIES who was born in 1725 and died in 1801, was a member of a well-known Aylsham family. Robert, his great-great grandfather had moved from Irstead to Aylsham in the early seventeenth century, and had bought lands from John Orwell, probably the man listed in the Rental as holding "a mess. with its appurts. . . built up in Myllgatestreete", one rood in area, in 1586. Robert himself appears in the Rental holding four acres of arable land in the East Field in the Millgate area in 1620. He is also the first Curties of many to be churchwardens of St.Michael's church, Aylsham.

The family continued to accumulate property in Aylsham in the next generation. Richard, Robert's second son, married Jane, daughter of Thomas Cressy. By the time he died in 1684, he owned the land called Orwells, property in Millgate, and thirty acres called Mucklins. (Munckeley in Eastonfield appears as a place-name in the Rental)

Richard's grandson, John Curties, whose memorial is on the floor of the nave in St.Michael's Church, was a weaver by trade. Later he became a grocer in Aylsham, and finally a tanner in Hanworth. He died in 1760, leaving a large family, including James, born in 1725, his third son.

While James's brothers became respectively, a tanner (John junior), a grocer (Thomas), and a weaver (Robert), James, also described as a grocer, consolidated the family lands in Millgate. Among the Millgate documents, there are papers relating to James's admission to two copyhold properties. The first, in 1766, is to ten acres, formerly owned by George Johnson, north of the River Bure and abutting upon the Aylsham to Tuttington Road, and the second, in 1773, is to three acres and one rood, formerly owned by Thomas Spurrell, miller. When Elizabeth Custans was in need of money in 1763, she mortgaged her estate to James Curties for £336, and in 1794, he was one of the Trustees of the Norwich to Cromer Turnpike Trust. He was clearly a man of substance.

James's will, drawn up in 1798, shows him taking great care in dividing his property among his nephews, great-nephews and nieces. He himself was a bachelor, and his brothers, John, Thomas and Robert, predeceased him. John's sons, Thomas and Robert, were given modest legacies. Robert's family had moved to Norwich, and, on his death, moved again to Northrepps, where his widow re-married. It was the family of Thomas, James's second brother, who were the chief beneficiaries of his will, perhaps because James and Thomas were both grocers, and both, as far as we know, lived the whole of their lives in Aylsham. Thomas junior, the eldest son, was left £200, but died before his uncle, so his legacy went to his daughter, Ann, who had in addition, £300 of her own. She married Thomas Plowright of King's Lynn, a member of the firm of ironmongers, Plowright & Pratt. John, the second son, was also left £200, and also predeceased his uncle, so the sum was shared between his daughter, Elizabeth and his son Thomas Grint Curties. Thomas senior's third son, Robert, had £150. The land which James had bought in 1766 and 1773 went to Stephen Ashley, a wine merchant of Aylsham, who had married one of James's nieces.

James died in 1801. By that time many of the younger generation had themselves died, or moved away from the town. The seventeenth and eighteenth centuries seem to have been the heyday of the Curties family in Aylsham. There was no Curties in Aylsham in the 1821 census.

The **HARVEY** and **BANE** families. - On the floor of the nave in St.Michael's Church, Aylsham, there is a tablet recording the death on June 9th.1770 of Thomas Spurrell, miller. Part of his estate was sold in 1771 to Thomas Harvey, millwright. It was copyhold

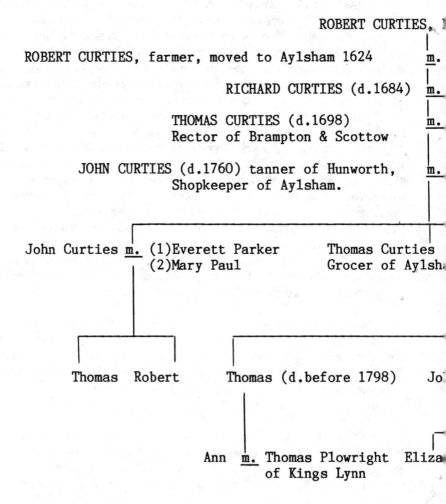

ROBERT CURTIES, 1

ROBERT CURTIES, farmer, moved to Aylsham 1624   m.

RICHARD CURTIES (d.1684)   m.

THOMAS CURTIES (d.1698)   m.
Rector of Brampton & Scottow

JOHN CURTIES (d.1760) tanner of Hunworth,   m.
Shopkeeper of Aylsham.

John Curties m. (1)Everett Parker   Thomas Curties
(2)Mary Paul   Grocer of Aylsh

Thomas   Robert   Thomas (d.before 1798)   Jo

Ann m. Thomas Plowright   Eliza
of Kings Lynn

Curties family: based on details from the family tree in
"Norfolk Ancestor" Vol.2 No.2 Sept. 1980 to which
acknowledgement is made

r of Irstead (d.1596)

abeth Goldney

Cressy (d.1688) daughter of Thomas Cressy of Aylsham

e Doughty, daughter of
Francis Doughty of Aylsham

y ? (d.1750)

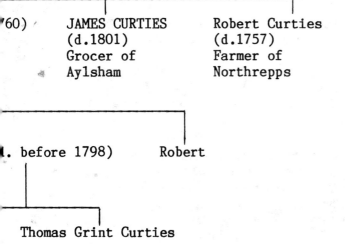

'60)   JAMES CURTIES   Robert Curties
         (d.1801)   (d.1757)
         Grocer of   Farmer of
         Aylsham   Northrepps

. before 1798)   Robert

    Thomas Grint Curties

land held from the Lord of the manor of Aylsham Wood, and is described as

> "all that messuage situate in Millgate Street in Aylesham. . .
> next the King's Highway leading to the bridge on the part
> of the west, and the street or way leading to the water mills
> on the north part. . . with the yard pump and garden to the
> same belonging. And also the barn and stable adjoining the
> said messuage. . .containing by estimation, 1 rood more or
> less, and also, all that close of arable land called or known
> by the name of Maiden's Bower, lying and being in Aylesham,
> aforesaid, next a horseway, leading to a meadow of the said
> Manor, on the part of the east; and a meadow called Pope's
> meadow, on the part of the west, and abutting upon the King's
> Highway leading from Aylesham aforesaid to Tuttington towards
> the North, and upon lands of the Lord of the said Manor towards
> the south, containing by estimation 1 acre and 1 rood more or
> less."

Thomas Harvey left these properties, and others which he had in Cromer, to his wife, Ann, for her lifetime. They were then to be sold by his executors, Thomas Drake of Aylsham, Gent. and John Pedder of Hevingham, farmer.

From a memorial tablet in the Baptist chapel in Aylsham, we discovered the relationship between Ann Harvey and John Pedder:

> 'In a vault beneath this tablet are deposited the remains
> of John Pedder, Gent. late of this parish
> who died the 7th.of January 1827 aged 78 years
> Also of Frances, his wife, who died
> the 5th.March 1831, aged 84 years.
>
> And also of Ann Harvey, her sister, who died
> the 16th.August 1822, aged 83 years.
> Anne Harvey and Frances Pedder were baptised
> in this parish, on a personal profession
> of Faith April 22nd. 1791 and became
> the founders of the Baptist Church in this place'
>
> "Peace to their memory"

Thomas Harvey, Ann's husband, made his will in 1798, and Ann was admitted to the lands in which she had a life interest the following year. She lived just long enough to be included as a householder living in Millgate in the 1821 census.

John Pedder, the surviving executor of Thomas Harvey's will, sold the estate to Robert Harvey in 1823. The Abstract of Robert's Title does not mention his relationship to Ann and Thomas. We think he was probably their son, although as a carver and gilder, he had chosen not to follow his father's occupation of millwright.

In time Robert, too, became a pillar of the Baptist church, and his epitaph records his death in 1842:

"For 50 years he was a zealous and devoted Christian
The last 12 of which he sustained the Deacon's office
in the church assembling in this place.
He rests from his Labours
and his works do follow him."

Robert's will is interesting, as it provides further evidence of family relationships. He left the property (excluding Maiden's Bower, which he had sold to Francis Parmeter in 1825) to his sister, Ann Harvey, for her life, and then to his other sister, Catherine Bane, wife of John Bane, 'Dissenting Minister'. After both sisters had died, the estate was to go to one of his executors, John Pedder Bane, millwright. The other executor was John Bane, and in 1846 we find them both described as living in Downham Market.

We think the family tree looks like this:-

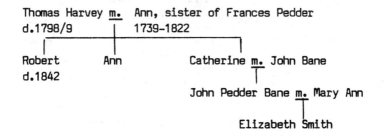

Thomas Harvey **m.** Ann, sister of Frances Pedder
d.1798/9   1739-1822

Robert   Ann   Catherine **m.** John Bane
d.1842

John Pedder Bane **m.** Mary Ann

Elizabeth Smith

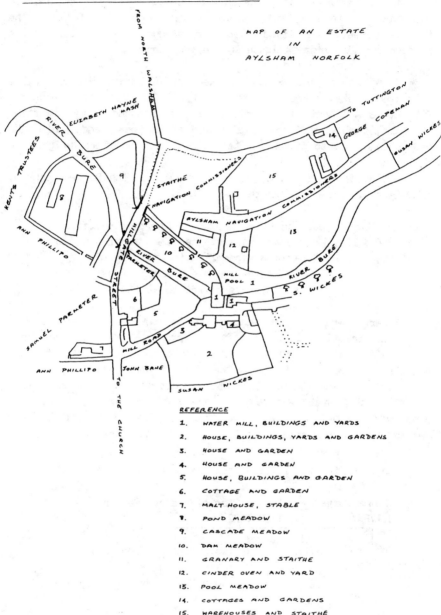

MAP OF AN ESTATE
IN
AYLSHAM NORFOLK

REFERENCE

1. WATER MILL, BUILDINGS AND YARDS
2. HOUSE, BUILDINGS, YARDS AND GARDENS
3. HOUSE AND GARDEN
4. HOUSE AND GARDEN
5. HOUSE, BUILDINGS AND GARDEN
6. COTTAGE AND GARDEN
7. MALT HOUSE, STABLE
8. POND MEADOW
9. CASCADE MEADOW
10. DAM MEADOW
11. GRANARY AND STAITHE
12. CINDER OVEN AND YARD
13. POOL MEADOW
14. COTTAGES AND GARDENS
15. WAREHOUSES AND STAITHE

42

A map drawn in February 1855 shows the property in the corner between Millgate and Mill Row, and gives the name of John Bane, presumably as trustee, as the owner. The land seems to have remained in the hands of the descendants of John Bane until 1950, when the representatives of John Pedder Bane's daughter, Mrs Elizabeth Smith, then deceased, sold it. Elizabeth had built a "villa" on the land in 1899, and this was No.46 Millgate in 1950.

JOHN FIELDE - was born about 1762, probably in Saxthorpe. He was listed twice in 1821 in the rough note book of William Morris, the Aylsham census enumerator. He occupied a house in Millgate with two women, presumably his wife, Ann, and his daughter, also called Ann. In addition, his name appears as the owner of three houses being built either in Workhouse Pightle, or "against Mr.Rackham's."

His first appearance in the Millgate Papers dates from 1820, and describes him as a millwright. A sale notice advertises two small pieces of land west of the road leading from Aylsham to Ingworth; one containing twenty perches and owned by Samuel and Ann Bircham and Robert Parmeter, and the other, of three acres and thirty five perches, owned by Thomas and Elizabeth Francis. On October 17th. 1820 John Fielde was admitted to these copyhold lands at the court of the Manor of Aylsham Lancaster. He followed this up in 1823 by buying a strip of land, twenty seven feet by ten feet in the same area, from John and Mary Warden.

His acquisitions were by no means confined to land west of the Cromer road. In the ten years from 1821-1831 he bought four properties in the Millgate area, all copyhold of the Manor of Aylsham Wood. In 1821 he paid Thomas Rackham and his daughter, Hannah, £427 for a messuage in Millgate - "wherein John Mash lately did, and John Fielde now lives, with outhouses, yard, garden and orchard", (presumably the property mentioned in the census, and already occupied by the Fieldes), and for two acres, one rood and twenty-two perches of arable land to the west of the house, and for a meadow of two acres and thirty-three perches north of the arable field. [Wright's Map: 330-333; 337-339?]. He added a strip of land, seventy-five yards in length and nine yards wide, south of Robert Parmeter's malthouse, in 1829, for which he paid Robert Parmeter £145 [Wright's Map: 329]

His other purchases in the Manor of Aylsham Wood were of land north of the River Bure. In 1830 he bought from the executors of the late John Steward two pieces of copyhold land containing together six acres, three roods and thirty perches between Tuttington Road on the south and the road "leading from the North Walsham road into the said Tuttington road on the east part" [Wright's Map: 391, 390 & 389?]. These lands were part of a holding of ten acres which John Tuck surrendered for £350 in 1817 to John Steward, defined "by an ancient description": five acres adjacent to Kirkhill Moor on the west, two acres called Bundalls abutting upon Kirkhill Moor on the east, another property not named, and three acres called Kirkhill. [Wright's Map: 391.390 & 389?]. The last purchase by John Fielde of which we have record was of four acres, one rood and twenty-two perches bought from James Hunt Holley in 1831 "to the use of Anne Fielde" [Wright's Map: 387]

John Fielde made his will in that year. He left all his property in Aylsham to his wife Ann for her life, and then to his daughter, Ann.

His executors were Robert William Parmeter, Gentleman, of Aylsham, and William Hase, Ironfounder, of Saxthorpe, and he left £30 to each of them for their trouble. The property he left in his will was valued at under £5,000. He left all his property in Saxthorpe to his daughter, Ann. In addition, he left £500 to be 'safely invested' to provide income for his wife, and a further £1,000 to be invested to provide income for his daughter. It looks as though John Fielde may have married a Miss Hase of Saxthorpe, and that this may explain in part his ability to accumulate his land holdings.

He died in 1837, and Mrs. and Miss Fielde were admitted by the Aylsham Lancaster Manor Court to the property west of the Ingworth road. In 1839, Ann, his daughter, now Mrs.Phillippo, wife of Matthias Phillippo, surgeon of Norwich, was admitted to the copyhold property that her father had held of the Manor of Aylsham Wood, 'expectant on the decease. . . of her mother'.

Mrs.Fielde died in 1847, and Ann Phillippo in 1868 or 1869. Ann's daughter, Ann Elizabeth Aldis of Eaton, Norwich, was admitted to all the land her grandfather had held in both Manors. After she died in 1905 the whole estate was sold to John Flaxman Daniels, an Aylsham farmer, by John Brown Aldis, widower, and his three children, all trustees under Ann Elizabeth's will. So the estate put together by John Fielde passed out of the hands of his descendants.

The WICKES family and the BELT Estate. On the east side of Millgate, behind the main street, lies the Belt Estate, bounded on the north by Mill Row and on the south by Sir William's Lane. White's Directory of 1836 names William Wickes of the Belt Estate as one of five landowners having 'neat mansions in the town', and as being owners of large portions of the parish.

The Wickes originally were tanners in Blickling. John Wickes, tanner, married Ruth, the daughter of Samuel Clarke, an Aylsham grocer and owner of the property called 'Paradise' near the church. They had two sons, Rice and William. The former inherited Paradise, and in 1814, the latter bought extensive property in Aylsham (139 acres including the Belt Estate) for £9,800. He acquired the property on the surrender of Benjamin Walker and his wife Sarah, who in turn had acquired it from James Beevor in 1804.

William Wickes and his wife Susan lived in the property in Millgate and had four children. The oldest of these, William Watts Wickes, inherited all the property on the death of his father in 1835. Their daughter, Ellen, married the Rev. W.W.Andrew of Ketteringham, whose stormy relationship with the squire is so delightfully told in "Victorian Miniature", by Owen Chadwick.

A tanyard is recorded by the river [No.58 in the 1839 Wright's map]. William Watts Wickes is not named as occupier of any of the premises in Millgate, although his mother is, but on his death, he is described as being 'gentleman of Aylsham'. He had no children, and the estate passed to the Andrew family, and in 1894, the Belt Estate was sold. It became the property of the Kerrisons of Burgh Hall, who finally sold it to the present owner, Mr. John Holman. Some of the land was compulsorily purchased in 1954 to provide land for the High School.

The Belt farmhouse carries a datestone of 1741, and the initials T R E in triangular form. It is said to have had the Georgian 'front' added in 1768. Access to the property is now via Mill Row. It was originally entered via the lodge at the junction of what is now Gas House Hill and Sir William's Lane.

The sale catalogue of 1894 describes the Belt "Residence and Grounds" as follows:

A house with modern stabling, Picturesque thatched cottage and garden, Thatched entrance lodge containing four rooms and outhouses and well, garden etc. occupied by the gardener. . . with grounds, woods, plantations etc. All in hand with possession at Michaelmas. Adjoining is a Valuable small farm in the occupation of Mr.Benjamin Cook, and two enclosures of land let to Mr.Starling. In all 209 acres 3 roods and 30 perches. [Abutments of the estate are listed with names of adjoining landlords.]

The WRIGHT family of boatbuilders and watermen. A study of the census returns from 1841-1881 revealed a number of men named Wright whose occupations were associated with the river, either as watermen, boatwrights or boatbuilders. Since our study was of the Millgate area only, some of the Wrights disappeared after only one entry; they may have moved to other parts of Aylsham, Norfolk, or further afield.

The best-known family of Wrights is that of the boatwright and boatbuilding family, starting with Thomas Wright, boatbuilder, listed in the Riches directory of 1843. An 1850 directory lists Robert and Thomas Wright, boatbuilders, and Kelly's Directory of 1883 lists Elijah Wright, boatbuilder of Millgate. There is also another large number of Wrights belonging to the family of Bartlett Wright, waterman.

BOATWRIGHTS & BOATBUILDERS: In the census of 1841, Thomas Wright, aged 50, a boatbuilder, of the Staithe, is listed with his wife, Mary and children Elizabeth [15] and James [12]. It is quite possible they had older children who had moved from the family home. Robert Wright [35] boatwright, living on the west side of Millgate, is listed with his wife, Elizabeth and five children.

The census of 1851, which gives more complete details, shows that Robert and Elizabeth have a further three children, and the older two have moved out. The full list of the children's names is:- Elizabeth, Robert, Mary, David, James, Annie, Harriet and Elijah. There is also a reference in the parish churchyard survey to two children who died in infancy - Thomas and Hannah.

Thomas Wright, boatbuilder, did not feature in the Millgate area in 1851. However, Geoffrey Nobbs in his article "Aylsham river in the last century",* refers to Thomas Wright, master boatbuilder, aged 62, as being listed in the 1851 census. There is also a Thomas Wright, waterman, aged 28 and married to Anne. He may be the son of Thomas Wright, boatbuilder. He was not listed in later census returns, but could be the Thomas Wright recorded as landlord of the Anchor Inn between 1868 and 1872 and also water bailiff during the same period.

By the 1871 census, Robert's three sons, David, James and Elijah have moved from the family home, and live with their wives in Millgate. They are listed as boatwrights (in 1861 as boat builders). There are no Thomases listed. The 1881 census does not list any of Robert's sons, only his daughter, Harriet Neale, living in Millgate with her husband. Robert has obviously died. A later Kelly's directory of 1883 lists Elijah Wright, boatbuilder, of Millgate. He was the youngest son of Robert, and perhaps had the advantage of being the only one there when his father became

*ALHS Journal & Newsletter. Vol.3 No.6. June 1992. pp173-178

elderly. After looking at details of the Aylsham population prepared for the 1821 census, it would seem very likely that Thomas and Robert were both sons of Thomas Wright of Millgate "towards the Mill," employed in trade.

WATERMEN: There was a Bartlett Wright in 1821 living in Millgate, listed as having two sons, and not being in trade. A second Bartlett Wright, waterman, living in Millgate, is noted in the census of 1851. He is absent, but his young wife Harriet, aged 19, and his son Bartlett are present. In 1861, Bartlett Wright is described as waterman - master rivercraft; his son, aged 12 is a waterman's assistant, and there are three more sons, Thomas, William and Frederick and baby Harriet. By 1881, Harriet Wright is a widow, charwoman, living in Mill Row, having had three more children. Her son, James [16] is described as a waterman. Frederick had been described as an agricultural labourer.

It is conceivable that the Bartlett Wright listed in 1821 is a younger brother of Thomas and Robert, and became a waterman because there was no room in the family business of boatbuilding, or because he preferred the mobile life on the river. Robert made sure that each of his sons had the skill of boatwright. His daughters married watermen or bricklayers.

It is recorded that Bob Wright built racing boats for the Aylsham Regatta in the mid 19th century. In the leaflet prepared by the Norfolk Museums Service we read that:

"The boatyards of Thomas and Robert Wright in the first half of the 19th century, and Elijah Wright in the second half, had achieved great distinction. One Aylsham-built wherry, named the Gypsy, had been sailed by her owner, Henry Doughty, on all the waterways of Europe, and her travels were recorded in his books."

Bob Wright's son, David, then aged 34, a boatwright, and married, is last noted in Millgate in 1871. He lived very near to his widowed father. One may conjecture that the forecasted coming of the railways made young men adapt their skills, and move from the river in the last part of the 19th century.

Chapter Eight

SEARCHING FOR THE NEW JERUSALEM

Although several of the Millgate personalities were referred to in the previous chapter, there are still others who require a chapter to themselves. These are the people whose lives were so closely interconnected that they need to be considered as a group. One such group is that of the Power, Berry and Clover families.

On the east side of Millgate, and south of Mill Row, is a group of small properties which are an interesting example of how, over a period of 150 years, the use of a site develops and changes in different hands. They also show how Millgate inhabitants were an integral part of the town, owning property and working in other areas, and contributing to its social and religious life. The properties are the present numbers 28-34 Millgate; the Stonemason's Arms, and numbers 42 and 44 Millgate. [Wright's map schedule Nos.305 and 306]

Our information starts with the marriage in 1743, of a John Power, farmer of Alby and "barber surgeon of Aylsham", to Ann Drosier of Banningham. She was the daughter of Edward Drosier, a tanner. They had three children; John, Mary and Ann. They planned to divide their properties (some of which were in other parts of Aylsham as well as Millgate) between the three children, but in the event, only Mary survived her parents, and as Mary Berry, widow of John Berry who had been Master of the Bridewell, she inherited all her parents' possessions in 1789. Their property in Millgate was described as two roods of land on which was one tenement, and later, two tenements or cottages, and adjoining pightle.

In 1820, Mary Berry died leaving all her property to the artist, Joseph Clover. He, in his turn, had inherited property in Millgate from his father, but by this time he was not living

50

Millgate in 1839.

there. It is interesting to speculate on why she did this, and we will come back to this later.

Around 1840, Joseph Clover sold all his Millgate properties to John Freeman, who was a stonemason and already resident in Millgate - the bond describes the transaction as "a bond for the quiet enjoyment of the property." Later, through a mortgage indenture of 1863, we find that John Freeman has had built, on the pightle of land, a public house with a stonemason's yard, outbuildings, yards and gardens. He also still held the two adjacent tenements previously described. His daughters later inherit and bought half each. Fanny Freeman, who later married Richard Chapman, paid £900 for four cottages (which had replaced the earlier two tenements) i.e. Nos. 28-34, the stonemason's yard, and the Stonemason's Arms, which by then had been let to Messrs. Bullard & Co. Her sister, married to Edmund Balls, executor of the property, retained land to the north and at some point they must have built Nos. 42 and 44. Richard Chapman and his children inherited the property, and when he died in 1926 the property (by this time one shop, three cottages and the stonemason's yard) was sold. Copies of the sale notices still exist. The properties were bought individually by Messrs. Pert, Dyball and Atkins. We do not know when the inn was sold.

Now to come back to Mary Berry and her bequest to Joseph Clover the artist. So far, our information has come from deeds in the 'Bishop bundles'. Other sources, including Clover family papers, have helped us to find possible reasons for her bequest, and at the same time, drawn our attention to certain happenings in the religious life of Aylsham.

The Clover family were well known in Aylsham and in Norwich. (Their frequent use of the Christian names Joseph and Thomas makes for identification problems at times.) Thomas Clover, son of a well-known Norwich farrier and veterinary surgeon, came to Aylsham, became a shopkeeper, married an Ann Barnard and lived in Millgate. This family were neighbours, and it would seem close friends of the Power family. It was this family friendship, lasting over many years, and spanning more than one generation which probably lay behind the bequest. Thomas and Ann had a large family, most of whom died young and are buried in the grave close by the charnel house in the churchyard. Three sons grew into adult life; one was Joseph, the artist (1779-1853) who trained as an engraver, and then became a portrait painter of some distinction, studying under Opie in London. He also exhibited at the annual exhibitions of the Norwich Society of Artists, founded by John Crome, and also, later, at the Royal Academy. He was betrothed to Mary Berry's daughter Ann, who died in 1801, aged 20. He remained a bachelor all his life.

The second son was John Wright Clover (1780-1865) who took over the family business, in 1803, on the corner of the Market Place and Hungate Street. He married twice; the first was a runaway marriage to Gretna Green with Elizabeth Taylor, the daughter of a Harleston clergyman. She died aged 28, leaving a daughter, Ann. He later married, (more advantageously perhaps!) the niece of John Bayfield Peterson - Elizabeth Mary Ann Peterson, who inherited Abbots Hall (known at that time as 'The Wood' Aylsham). They had a number of children, the most eminent of whom was the pioneer anaesthetist, Joseph Clover, recently commemorated by a plaque on the wall of the new King Chemist building on the site of the former Clover shop in the Market Place.

The third son was Thomas (1781-?) a farmer in Colby, who married Maria Cook in 1804 and had a number of children.

The other link between these two families was a religious one, and came to light when, in the course of investigating the extent and whereabouts of Mary Berry's property in the town, it was discovered that in 1796 she had bought a Meeting House! From the Clover family papers, from letters and other records, it is clear that the Meeting House was to be used as a New Jerusalem Church according to the beliefs of a religious group called Swedenborgians. This sect were followers of Emanuel Swedenborg who was a Swedish scientist and writer during the eighteenth century. The writings of Emanuel Swedenborg seem to have attracted interest amongst artists and literary figures including William

Blake (for a short time only), John Flaxman, Elizabeth Barrett Browning and Helen Keller. The congregations were called the New Jerusalem Church, and clergy and ministers from different denominations were involved in starting them in different parts of the country. John Wright Clover was closely involved in Aylsham and Joseph Clover was closely associated with the London church, and was a trustee from 1822-26. From other sources, it would seem that his father, and probably an uncle in Norwich, were associated with the starting of the Norwich church in 1801.

Where was this Meeting House? A bond of 1796, recording the transaction between Mary Berry and a John Boardman reads:

"All that new erected Meeting House situate in Aylsham including seats, pews and other features now standing and being therein, and also all that cottage or West End of a tenement situate in Aylsham aforesaid, near the said Meeting House, and now in the occupation of William Shreeve; and also all those pieces and parcels of land adjoining and belonging to the said premises, or to some part thereof".

Her daughter Ann [died 1801], Thomas Wright Clover [died 1803] and Dr.Saunders, an Aylsham surgeon, became trustees. From the Aylsham Lancaster Manor Court Books, we know that the building was in existence in 1791, having been erected on land belonging to a Richard Jex and his wife, and surrendered by him to John Boardman of Gorleston, from whom it passed into the possession of Mary Berry. The Manor Court Rolls describe in detail the 'pieces and parcels of land' mentioned in the bond. They include a cottage and a long passage way next to the east end of the cottage leading from a gateway from the street on the north to the Meeting House. The description of the Meeting House and land closely resembles the present Baptist church and its situation, and its description in the Baptist Bicentenary Booklet of 1991. Recent measurements have confirmed that the oldest part of the present Baptist Church must have been the Meeting House bought by Mary Berry.

There are certain other significant dates, facts and events which make interesting reading, and create a picture of the life of the various dissenting communities in Aylsham which is at once confusing, intriguing and needs interpreting:-

1] In 1789, we learn from the Dissenter Meeting Houses register that a Richard Jex was licensed to hold dissenters' meetings on his premises, described as a 'former combing house' converted into a schoolroom.

2] By 1791, we know that the new Meeting House had been erected.

Methodist tradition has it, that it was built by the Methodists, and licensed in the name of Rev.Thos.Tattersall of Norwich, named in Charles Wesley's records. By 1842, they had sold it to the Baptists, having built the new Methodist Chapel on the roadside in White Hart Street. The Aylsham Baptists' Bicentenary Booklet notes that the Rev. Joseph Kinghorn, from Norwich, started the Baptist Church in Aylsham by the baptism of five believers in the River Bure, in April 1791. Mention is made in a Norwich Baptist Minute Book of members going to Aylsham in 1787. They believe that the Meeting House was built by a Baptist 'speculative' builder, called Wilks, and that he allowed the Rev.Joseph Kinghorn to use it. Maybe he allowed the Methodists to use it, too, or vice versa?

We know from Browne's "History of Congregationalism" that in 1791 the Rev.Samuel Crowther from Clare in Suffolk, was ordained minister of the Independent (Congregational) Chapel or Meeting House in Oulton. He is known to have preached in Aylsham on a number of occasions, and to have formed a congregation there which, after a short time, combined with the congregation in Oulton. We know also that he was married a year or two later to a Mary Boardman and some years later still, to a Susannah Boardman.

In 1791, as noted above, possession of the Meeting House, according to Manor Court Rolls, passed from Richard Jex to John Boardman of Gorleston.

3] The next significant date seems to be 1796, when Mary Berry purchased the Meeting House from John Boardman (whose interest and role in all this is so far not known - he may have had Baptist interests). Her interest, however, is very clear. There exist two letters written by Mrs.Berry, one to a Mr. Clover (presumably J.W.) in 1798, and another (not addressed) in 1804, showing her commitment to the New Jerusalem Church. She covenants to surrender the church to its trustees, and expressly states that she wishes to ensure that no one should be expected to contribute financially to its upkeep, unless they can afford to do so. She wants to arrange instruction for two poor children of parents interested in the New Church (to be chosen by Mr.Clover), and she is prepared to make books available for their instruction, which could later be passed on to other deserving children. She refers, in the earlier letter, to a Mr.Crowther as the person she expects may undertake the teaching. Was he the same Mr.Crowther as the minister at Oulton?

In the same year, the Rev.Joseph Kinghorn is said to have applied to the Baptist Fund for financial assistance, but it is not clear if he got it. He was granted possession of the land and building in 1811 by the Norwich courts as a result of disturbances against nonconformists in the town.

The picture that emerges is one of much activity in a number of nonconformist groups in the town at the end of the 18th.century. Perhaps more than one was allowed to use the Meeting House, the first to be 'purpose-built' in the town, as opposed to meeting in private houses under licence, a practice which continued until well into the 19th.century. Deeds and Court Rolls show who owns a property, but do not necessarily tell us which denomination they represent. Perhaps, too, the denominations were not as distinct, or as separate as we tend to think of them now. There is reference in the Clover papers to the fact that 'J.W.' and his wife continue to attend the parish church, and we know that Mary Berry was buried in the churchyard of St.Michael's. We do not yet know when the New Jerusalem Church in Aylsham ceased to meet.

---ooOoo---

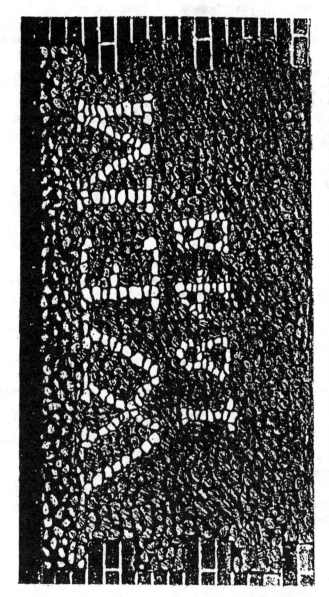

INITIALS AND DATE ON FRONT FACADE OF 1 & 2 MASH'S ROW

Chapter Nine

MASH'S ROW, MILLGATE   1845-1992
AND THE MASH FAMILY   1741-1914

In 1845, William Mash built a row of six red brick and flint cottages, which were known as Mash's Row, on land at the end of Millgate, near to the River Bure and Drabblegate. This area of land is referred to as Cascade Meadow, No.529 on the 1839 Wright's map schedule.   A plaque with Freehold, W.E.M. 1845 is attached to the back wall of one of the cottages, and the initials are those of William and his wife, Elizabeth Hayne Mash.

Each cottage had two small rooms on the ground floor, and two of an equal size on the upper floor, with a staircase connecting both floors.   There were no bathrooms, and water for domestic purposes was drawn from a well. At the rear of each cottage there was a garden which extended to the banks of an outlet from the River Bure and, on the other side of the lane, another garden which was used for growing vegetables and soft fruit. Each cottage had a lavatory closet at the rear of the garden. The well which served the cottages was situated near to the lane in the garden of 5 Mash's Row.

Three years later, William Mash had a house built on the Millgate street side of the same piece of land. Rumour has it that the house was originally built as a public house, but never used as such, and was occupied as one private dwelling, and subsequently converted into two semi-detached houses. The original house was square, two storeys high, with a front facade of red bricks and grey sea coast flints, in the centre of which, between the two halves of the building in small cream coloured stones, are the initials W.E.M. and the date 1848.   Each house has a door with a plain portico, placed at the end of the building, and two rectangular sash windows with small panes of glass, near the centre.   Both sides of the original building reflected the front facade, but the back wall of the house was constructed from red bricks and large coarse flints. There is no doubt that the front appearance of the building was of greater importance than the back.

The original layout of the rooms in the house is now difficult to define, since the conversion to two separate houses, but it would appear to have had four rooms downstairs, with access through a doorway between the two front rooms. This arrangement was duplicated on the floor above. At the time of conversion, the door on the ground floor was removed and the space filled in. On the upper floor, a brick wall was built on one side, in the first house, leaving the door and frame still in position on the other side. A staircase linked both floors, and a new staircase was put in at the time of conversion. There was also another small staircase in the second house, which led to a small, window-less room in the loft.

In common with houses of this period, there was no bathroom, water came from a well and there was an outside closet. Both houses had front and rear gardens, and each one had a further garden on the far side of Mash's Row. The houses were deemed to be in Millgate until the 1980s when they were officially classified as numbers 1 & 2 Mash's Row, and the cottages 3 - 8 Mash's Row.

In the 19th.century a one-storey brick extension with a sloping pantile roof was built on to the side of No.2 Mash's Row. In 1914, the tenant was a Mr.J.Tight, a fishmonger, who had a small smokehouse at the end of the rear garden, and sold fish to customers from the front part of the extension. In 1952, this extension was altered to the full height of the house, almost doubling it in size. The secondary front door was removed in the process, a large window was inserted and the front wall was made to match the original. A small brick lean-to had been added to the rear of No.1, which was used as a kitchen, and was demolished in 1978 when a two-storey extension was built at the rear of the house. The side wall of this extension was made to match the original. When the foundations for this extension were being dug, a well, which had been bricked over, was discovered a few yards from the back of the original building. This well had been used when the house was first occupied, and had subsequently been filled in and forgotten.

58

A long, low building, 50 feet by 12 feet, with an earth floor had been built at the rear of 2 Mash's Row, and it is rumoured that it was intended as a skittle alley for the public house. It was first described as a cart shed and stable, and later referred to as a barn. The barn remained in its original form until 1965 when part of it was taken down to make a conservatory and a concrete floor laid in this area, but it was not until 1991 that all the earth floor in the barn was concreted.

At the Staithe, and near to No.1 Mash's Row, there was a small blacksmith's forge. James Martin is on record as being the blacksmith in 1858, and living in the house with his family. By 1879, John Martin and his son are listed as blacksmiths with a further forge at Burgh. John Martin was succeeded by his son, Walter John Martin at both the Staithe and at Burgh in 1892. During the 1914-1918 war, troops were billeted near to the mill, and the military horses were shod by a blacksmith at the Staithe. The forge was abandoned between the wars and fell into disrepair, and was rebuilt as a double garage in the 1970s.

William Mash died at the early age of forty-nine in 1849. Ownership of the houses and cottages in Mash's Row passed to his wife, Elizabeth Hayne Mash, and then in 1874, to their son, Henry Brett Mash. He left Mash's Row to his sister, Katherine Howlett, for her lifetime, and on her death in 1914, all the property was auctioned including the houses and cottages in Mash's Row. Ownership of Mash's Row passed out of the hands of the Mash family at this time. The auction was held at the Black Boys in Aylsham on 28th.July 1914. Charles Henry Rooke, a retired innkeeper of Drabblegate, bought 1 and 2 Mash's Row as a double dwelling house with stable, cartshed, outbuildings, yards and gardens. The tenants at the time were Mr.Tight and Mr.Matthews. The six cottages were bought by a Mr.Frank Searle.

The tenants living in Mash's Row in the second part of the nineteenth century, had a variety of occupations - agricultural labourer, coal porter, journeyman miller, dressmaker, boat riveter, harness maker, labourer at the gas works, wherryman and warrener.

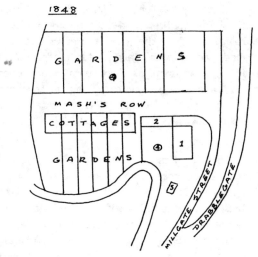

1848

1. HOUSE
2. CARTSHED AND STABLE
3. BLACKSMITH'S FORGE
4. WELL

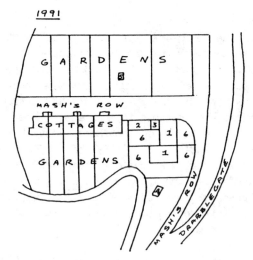

1991

1. HOUSE
2. BARN
3. CONSERVATORY
4. DOUBLE GARAGE
5. GARAGE
6. GARDEN

Tenancy often passed from father to son or daughter. Neither Charles Henry Rooke, nor Frank Searle lived in any of the properties after their purchase, but they rented them out to tenants.

In 1929, Charles Henry Rooke died, and in his will he left 1 and 2 Mash's Row in trust for his grandson, Archer Albert Woods, until he attained the age of 21. The tenants at the time were John Matthews and Walter Johnson. On the 29th.December 1936, Archer Woods, by then an Able Seaman serving on HMS Caledon in Devonport, came of age and inherited his property. Eight months later, he sold Nos. 1 & 2 Mash's Row to Harold Matthews, a craftsman builder, who later built both of the extensions on to the houses, and converted a part of the barn into a conservatory.

The six cottages in Mash's Row had, by 1937, passed from the ownership of Frank Searle to Arthur Edward Partridge, an Aylsham butcher. They were sold again to Frederick Breese. The interiors of these cottages remained basically unchanged, until a combined shower-room and toilet was installed on the ground floor of each one. Numbers 3 & 4 have been converted into one dwelling, and an extension has been built on to the side of the last cottage.

Aylsham residents in the 18th and 19th centuries were dependent on wells for their water supply and it was often far from pure. The quality of water in the town became a matter of some concern when fourteen cases of typhoid fever were reported in the town in 1904. Clean water was eventually piped in from Norwich City Waterworks as recently as 1938, and even then Mash's Row was not immediately connected to the mains, and for a time a standpipe was provided for the resident's use. The same situation applied to drainage, and Mash's Row was one of the last places in Aylsham to be connected to the mains system in the 1950s. As for lighting, although a gas supply existed in the town from 1850, this never reached Mash's Row, and paraffin lamps continued to be used until electricity was eventually installed in the early 1930s.

Aylsham Town Station at the end of Millgate, near to Mash's Row, was opened in 1883 by the Eastern & Midland Railway which later became the Midland & Great Northern Railway. Many residents of Aylsham who used this station would cycle to Mash's Row, and for a small fee, leave their bicycles at the blacksmith's shop, and collect them on their return to cycle home. This line was closed down in 1959, the station demolished and the area left as an open space, part of which has been incorporated into the Weavers' Way.

The land on which the houses and cottages of Mash's Row stand is close to the River Bure. Long before William Mash built his properties, this area must have been subject to flooding, whenever the river ran high after an excess of rain. There is no documentation on any flooding of this area until the flood in August 1912. It had rained every day for a fortnight, and this was followed on the 26th.August by $7\frac{1}{2}$ inches of rain, with $6\frac{1}{2}$ inches falling in twelve hours. The river overflowed its banks, and Mash's Row was flooded with the water reaching the first floor level of the dwellings, and the residents had to be rescued by boat. There was widespread flooding all over the area, which destroyed crops, drowned animals, brought down trees and telegraph poles, and swept away bridges. On either side of the railway at Drabblegate, the meadows were flooded, and a portion of the embankment was washed away leaving the rails suspended over the gap. When the occupants of Mash's Row were eventually able to return, they were faced with the heartbreaking task of cleaning the mud out of their homes. A considerable amount of household goods had been destroyed or damaged by the force of the water sweeping through the buildings. A relief fund was opened by the County and the generous subscriptions enabled money to be distributed to all of those who had suffered loss or damage.

In recent years there have been further floods in Mash's Row, the last one occurring in 1986 after heavy rain. One of the mills higher up the river Bure did not open its flood gates to allow the water to flow through. Consequently, when they were opened, the heavy volume of water broke the banks at Ingworth, flooded meadows in its path, and eventually reached Mash's Row. Following this flood, the River Authority dredged the bed of the river, and cleared the edges of rushes and weeds.

The houses and cottages built by William Mash in Mash's Row are now listed as Grade II buildings. They are a part of Aylsham's heritage, and are protected for the future in a conservation area.

So much for the buildings in Mash's Row, now let us look at the man himself, William Mash, who was responsible for their existence, and also look at his family.

THE MASH FAMILY OF AYLSHAM, 1741-1914

John Mash was born in 1773. His father's first name is unknown. His mother, Elizabeth, was born in 1741, and after the death of her first husband, married a man called Smith. John Mash's wife was also called Elizabeth and was born in 1771. John and Elizabeth had four children - Elizabeth in 1796, followed by Mary Ann in 1798, John Drake in 1799 and William in 1800. The Aylsham Poor Rate books for the years 1814-1823 show that John Mash had a farm, and rented glebe land from the Rev.N.V.Pitman and the Rev.Norris. He also had a malt house.

Mary Ann, the daughter of John and Elizabeth, died on 23rd.February 1816, at the age of eighteen, and is buried in St.Michael's churchyard in Aylsham. Six years later, on 11th.October 1822, Elizabeth, their eldest daughter, died aged twenty-six, and was buried in St.George's Burial Ground, Bloomsbury, London. John Mash died on the 13th. October 1833 aged sixty years, and was followed on the 2nd. December by his eldest son, John Drake Mash aged thirty-four. Both were buried in the same grave as Mary Ann in St.Michael's churchyard. John Mash's wife outlived both her husband and children, and died in 1856 in her eighty-fifth year, and is interred in the family grave.

William Mash, like his father, was a farmer, and at the age of 23 had his own farm. On the 4th. May 1831, at the Court of Aylsham Lancaster, Thomas Stoneham, a baker of Aylsham, agreed to pay £500 plus interest, for a dwellinghouse owned by William

Mash. There is no record of where this property was situated, but it is possibly the first of William Mash's speculative deals to raise money to buy or rent additional land. On 2nd. May 1836, William Mash was again before the Court of Aylsham Lancaster, when he presented the will of Sarah Gunner, a spinster of Aylsham. This will dated 17th. November 1835 left:-

'all my messuages, lands, tenements and hereditaments in Aylsham . . . to William Mash of Aylsham, yeoman, his heirs. and assigns for ever'

The property that William inherited from Sarah Gunner was situated behind Red Lion Street. Why Sarah Gunner left her property to William is not known, but she could have been a relative. In the same year of 1836, William Mash also rented the Anchor Inn in Aylsham from the brewery company of William Bircham. He appears to have expanded his activities from his small farm in 1823, to acquiring further land and property, and these are shown in the Rate Books for the years 1837-1841. In 1837, he rented land from W.Wilson in the Walsham Road; three plots from the Rev. Hunt; a house and land on the Walsham Road from I.Clearwaller, and he owned land that had lately belonged to Copeman Taylor. He also rented land near Banningham from W.H.Windham, in 1840.

The schedules to the 1839 Wright's map of Aylsham gives the following list of William Mash's properties:-

No.on plan	Occupier	Description
209	Jonathan Burrell	Cottages
324	W.Mash	Shed & yard
403	W.Mash	Copeman Taylor's Piece
404	W.Mash	waste
520	W.Mash	Cascade Piece
529	W.Mash	Cascade Meadow
303	W.Mash	Cottages & gardens.

The property 209 refers to the cottages left to William Mash by Sarah Gunner in 1836, and were obviously let at that time to Jonathan Burrell.

324 lay behind the Anchor Inn, and 403 consisted of more than six acres of arable land, while 404 is described as wasteland, and both were situated at Drabblegate.

520 refers to an area of arable land between Drabblegate and Banningham Road.

529 is described as meadow land, situated at the far end of Millgate, near to Drabblegate, bounded on one side by the River Bure and the outlet that flowed to the mill.

303 refers to cottages in Millgate.

All this property and land was estimated at 14 acres, 1 rood, 19 perches, and the rate paid was £5-0-6d. The Poor Rate book of 1841 shows that William Mash rented the land of Sexton's Field and Copeman Taylor's Piece from William Wilson, but they were co-owners one year later.

William Mash married Elizabeth Hayne Brett. She was born on 23rd.December 1804 at Swanton Abbott, and was the daughter of William Brett and his wife Anne Hayne. William and Elizabeth Hayne Mash had four children who died in infancy and are buried in the grave of their grandparents, John and Elizabeth Mash. On the 1st.August 1843, a daughter Katherine was born, followed by a son Henry Brett, on the 17th. March 1845. Both of these children were born in Aylsham and survived to adulthood.

From 1836-1846, William Mash is recorded as the innkeeper of the Anchor Inn in Aylsham. In addition to being an innkeeper, he continued to farm the land that he owned or rented. In 1845, he either erected new cottages, or renovated those that were already there on a site that he owned in Millgate. These flint and brick cottages are numbers 2, 4 and 6 in Millgate, and on the facade of one of them there is a small plaque with the initials W.E.M. and the date 1845. The initials are those of William and his wife Elizabeth. In this same year, he developed the meadow that he owned near the bottom end of Millgate, by erecting a row of six flint and brick cottages; these were named Mash's Row. The house that he built three years later, next to the cottages, is thought to have been built as a public house, and William Mash having been the landlord of the Anchor Inn possibly intended having his own inn. However, it was never used as a public house.

PLAQUE ON COTTAGES
2,4 & 6 MILLGATE

PLAQUE ON COTTAGES
IN MASH'S ROW

William Mash died on the 24th.March 1849 at the early age of forty-nine years, and is buried in St.Michaels churchyard in Aylsham. He left a forty-five year old widow, a daughter Katherine aged six years, and a son, Henry Brett, who was four at the time of his father's death. All the research to find the will of William Mash has so far been unsuccessful, and it may be that he did not make one. His son, Henry Brett Mash, was regarded as his heir, and until he became of age all the properties owned by his father were administered by his mother, Elizabeth Hayne Mash. She continued to farm the land until 1854 and maintained the properties of William Mash, for her son who would inherit them when he became of age.

At a Manor Court, on 30th.April 1851, Henry Brett Mash was admitted to the property of the Stone House in Millgate, with gardens of an estimated half acre. In the same court he was acknowledged as owning one rood of land formerly called Church Close, which his father had acquired in 1826 on the surrender of Robert Mack and his wife, Mary.

The 1861 census lists Elizabeth Hayne Mash as a house proprietor, living in Millgate with her sixteen year old daughter, Katherine, who was a dressmaker. The Valuation list of properties for Aylsham in 1864 records that Elizabeth was the owner of a house

66

in Millgate, six cottages near the Staithe, eight cottages in Millgate, and two near Red Lion Street. The latter two cottages refer to those inherited by William Mash from Sarah Gunner. She also owned six acres of land on the Walsham Road, which were rented by Robert Bartram in 1867, and land and cottages amounting to six acres tenanted by John Nicholls.

The 1871 census refers to Elizabeth as a lodging-house keeper in Millgate, living in the Stone House with Katherine, who was twenty seven years old and still employed as a dressmaker. By 1874, Henry Brett Mash had inherited all the properties in Millgate and Mash's Row, but what happened to the land that his mother owned in the Walsham Road, the land and cottages rented by John Nicholls and the cottages behind Red Lion Street, remains a mystery as they were not passed on. Elizabeth Hayne Mash died in Aylsham in 1883 at the age of seventy-eight.

Henry Brett Mash became an Inspector of Lodging Houses and an Inspector under the Petroleum Act in Downham Market. He was also a Superintendent of Police and the Deputy Chief Constable for Norfolk. He died at Downham Market on 20th.March 1912 aged sixty-seven years. In his will, drawn up in 1909, he left £2154.17.11d and directed that all his property should be left to his sister Katherine Howlett (nee Mash) for her lifetime. After her death, the properties were to be sold by the executors, Walter Bailey, (his brother-in-law) and Frank Searle (a County Solicitor's Clerk) and the monies left in trust for the child or children of his stepson, John Arthur Kidd, for when they attained the age of twenty-one years.

Katherine Howlett, a widow and the sister of Henry Brett Mash, died in 1914, aged 72, at Sidcup in Kent. In her will, Katherine left various small sums of money to friends, and £150 to her cousin Sophia, the wife of William Millett, a blacksmith of Sparham. To John Kidd, the son of her sister-in-law Nancy Mash, she left Henry Brett Mash's presentation clock, her candelabra, and £50 to his wife Kate. After other small bequests, the residue of the estate was divided between her six cousins, Sophia Millett, Emily Calaby, Mary Parker, Annie Maria Howard, Ada Feltham Cord Nutman and Benivento Nutman.

AYLSHAM.

STANLEY W. BRUCE is favoured with instructions from the Executor of the Will of the late Mr. Henry Brett Mash, to Sell by Public Auction, at the Black Boys Hotel, Aylsham, on TUESDAY, the 28th JULY, 1914, at Four o'clock in the Afternoon, precisely, the following valuable

FREEHOLD PROPERTY

In Aylsham, in the undermentioned or such other Lots as may be determined upon at the Sale, namely :—

Lot 1. All those Six well-built BRICK and STONE COTTAGES, with out-houses and gardens, in Millgate Street, on Gas House Hill, in the occupation of Mr. King and others at gross rentals of £32 15s. per annum.

Lot 2. All those Three well-built BRICK and STONE COTTAGES, with outhouses and gardens, in Millgate Street, adjoining Lot 1, in the occupation of Mr. Randell and others, at gross rentals of £15 12s. per annum. There is a well of good water for the above nine cottages.

Lot 3. All that substantially built DWELLING-HOUSE now known as "-STONE HOUSE," containing 6 Bedrooms, 4 Lower Rooms, Cellar, and Wash House, with a very good Garden, also Pump for hard and soft water, in Millgate Street, Gas House Hill, in the occupation of Mrs. Braithwaite, at a rental of £15 per annum.

Lot 4. All those Two conveniently built BRICK and STONE MESSUAGES with Gardens and Outbuildings, comprising Stable, and Cart Shed, in Millgate Street, facing the Midland and Great Northern Railway, now or lately occupied by Mr. J. Tight and Mrs. Martin, at a gross rental of £16 per annum.

Lot 5. All those Six well-built BRICK and STONE MESSUAGES with Out-houses and Gardens now known as "Mash's Row," with Small Piece of Land (about 0a. 1r. 14p.), near thereto, and used as a drying ground, in Millgate Street, in the occupation of Mr. R. Pratt and others, at gross rentals of £31 10s. per annum. There is a pump with a good supply of water, for Lots 4 and 5.

For Further Particulars, apply to the Auctioneer, Bank Street, Aylsham, or to

MR. C. ERNEST JACKSON,
Solicitor,
The Crescent, Wisbech

On 28th.July 1914, all the properties that had belonged to Henry Brett Mash were auctioned at the Black Boys Hotel, Aylsham. They were sold as five lots:-

Lot.1   Six brick and stone cottages with out-houses and gardens in Millgate St. on Gas House Hill.

Lot.2   Three brick and stone cottages with out-houses and gardens in Millgate - adjoining Lot 1.

Lot.3   A dwelling house known as the 'Stone House'.

Lot.4   Two brick and stone messuages with gardens and out-buildings, comprising stable and cart shed in Millgate.

Lot.5   Six brick and stone messuages with out-houses and gardens now known as Mash's Row.

For present day references, these are as follows:-

Lot.1 = 2 - 12 Millgate. [Numbers 8-12 have been converted into two dwellings and No.10 no longer exists.]
Lot.2 = 14, 16 and 18 Millgate.
Lot.3 = The 'Stone House', 20 Millgate.
Lot.4 = 1 & 2 Mash's Row.
Lot.5 = 3 - 8 Mash's Row.

Henry Brett Mash's brother-in-law, Walter Bailey had died in London in June 1912, and Frank Searle, the remaining trustee, was responsible for the sale. He bought Lot 5 in the auction, and retained this property until it came into the ownership of Arthur Edward Partridge in 1937. Lot 4 was bought by Charles Henry Rooke, Lot.3 the Stone House, was bought by C.H.Meale and then sold to James Flaxman Bond, who later sold it in 1920 to Francis Southgate, a retired Superintendent of Police. The buyers of Lots 1 and 2 are unknown.

The properties and farm lands that William Mash acquired in and around Aylsham have now been dispersed to individual farmers and property owners. This particular line of the Mash family has died out, as neither Henry Brett Mash nor his sister Katherine had any children. All that is left of the family are references in a few old books and documents, the gravestones in St.Michael's churchyard and the initials W.E.M. on the houses and cottages in Millgate and Mash's Row.

THE MASH FAMILY

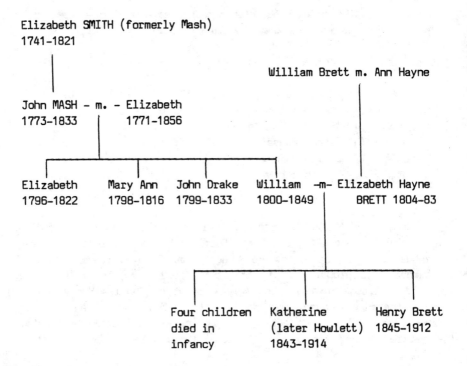

Elizabeth SMITH (formerly Mash)
1741-1821

William Brett m. Ann Hayne

John MASH - m. - Elizabeth
1773-1833   1771-1856

| Elizabeth | Mary Ann | John Drake | William | —m— Elizabeth Hayne |
| 1796-1822 | 1798-1816 | 1799-1833 | 1800-1849 | BRETT 1804-83 |

Four children
died in
infancy

Katherine
(later Howlett)
1843-1914

Henry Brett
1845-1912

Chapter Ten

THE ANCHOR INN

It is a trifle ironic that none of the documents in the 'Bishop bundles', which were loaned to the history group by Mr.Tom Bishop, to further our knowledge of Millgate history, threw any additional light on the history of his own home in Bridge House, or on its previous existence as the Anchor Inn. The property's connection with the Parmeter family, however, has made it possible to learn something of its history from other sources.

The first known reference to this property as an inn is in 1793, when it was left by Robert Parmeter the Elder, miller and flour merchant, to his daughter, Ann Lungley, who was the wife of Isaac Lungley, a farmer in Boxford, Suffolk. It was described as "the Public House in Millgate Street, near the bridge, called the sign of the Anchor; together with three cottages to the same adjoining". With it went a piece of land (Pond Meadow) and a piece of pasture land lying on the east side of the river opposite Pond Meadow. There is one other reference to the inn, in the same year, in the United British Directory of 1793, where a John Jennings is recorded as 'victualler'.

Robert Parmeter is known to have bought the property in 1771 from the executors of Thomas Spurrell, miller. It was described then as - "those two messuages adjoining, situate near the bridge in Millgate Street in Aylsham, wherein Hammond Beaton, John Beaton and John Smith now live, and yards and gardens adjoining". With it went a meadow called Pond Meadow, adjoining in part to the yards and gardens of the said messuage (1 acre and 3 roods) in the occupation of Michael Francis, and meadowland on the east side of the river, opposite the last mentioned meadow ($\frac{1}{2}$ acre) in the use of Thomas Harvey. The manor court roll goes on to comment that these premises were those to which - "by different description the said Thomas Spurrell was admitted on the surrender of John Webster and his wife, Hannah, in 1753."

Bridge House, formerly the Anchor Inn.

The Websters acquired the property through Hannah's father, Henry Wymarke, who bequeathed it to his two daughters in 1746. When it was surrendered to William Spurrell, the description in the manor court roll is of - "16 perches of land with a messuage thereon built, parcel of the Toft Epp; 3 roods of Korrodale otherwise Kurdole, parcel of the said Toft lying next the Great Bridge of Aylsham; ½ acre of land parcel also of the same Toft Epp in Aylsham aforesaid".

We know, therefore, that the property was in existence before 1746, and that it seems to have become a public house between 1771 and 1793, presumably to serve the increased river traffic associated with the Navigation.

In 1830 William Wilson was the innkeeper. In 1833, the property was purchased by Birchams, the Reepham brewers, and in 1836, William Mash, builder and farmer, became the innkeeper and remained so until 1846, three years before his death. James Fitt was the innkeeper between 1850 and 1858. During his time the Aylsham Aquatic Club was formed (on 9th. May 1851) and based itself at the Anchor Inn. The first president was Samuel Parmeter.

In the Aylsham directories, between 1858 and 1868, Robert Easton is listed as the landlord. Curiously enough, the 1864 directory refers to the inn as the "Hope & Anchor". Still relying on the directories, we have Thomas Wright recorded as landlord between 1868 and 1872. Wright was also the water bailiff during that period. From 1875 to 1888, Thomas Read was landlord, aided by his wife, Mary Ann Read.

In 1878, the Birchams sold the Anchor Inn to Steward & Pattesons, the Norwich and Ely brewers. The Statutory Declaration made at that time by William Bircham and Francis Parmeter describes the property as being a public house, with stabling, a skittle ground, a large garden bounded by the river, and three cottages adjoining with gardens behind. "One of these cottages was many years ago converted into a bakehouse, but is not now used as such, and it is now attached to the public house, and used as a Herring Curing House". Francis Parmeter was the son of Robert Parmeter the

Younger, described as "beer brewer", who lived at Booton Hall.

In the Sale notice of 1878, it forms lot 16, and the description includes the following:- "A carrier's house, just outside the town, on the road from North Walsham, containing large parlour, good Tap, and Bar; stone-paved cellar, kitchen and store room; four bedrooms and two attics; yard in rear, with gates to road, in which is stabling for about twenty horses, and skittle ground; also a good garden, bounded by the river. etc." The Herring Curing house obviously continued for some time, as in 1892 James Tight is listed as landlord and also as "fish curer".

There must be many gaps in the list of names of successive landlords, but we know from directories that Ernest Clarke was a landlord for a considerable period. He is listed from 1916 at least, right up to 1937 when the county directories ceased to be published, and it is possible he went on for much longer than that date. During World War Two, the Anchor Inn became one of the favourite watering holes for servicemen in the Royal Canadian Airforce stationed at Oulton. The Canadian, Murray Peden, author of the book "A thousand shall fall" which recounts his life at the Oulton base, recalls sitting in the bar of the Anchor, where the landlady, Mrs. Ena Wilson, let them play through her large collection of Bing Crosby records.

Bridge House ceased to be the Anchor Inn sometime after the end of the Second World War. At least one of our committee members can remember enjoying a drink there. In 1962 the property was acquired by Mr.Tom Bishop and is now a private house.

Through the many deeds and documents acquired by Mr.Bishop, and generously loaned by him to the Local History Society, we have been stimulated into digging into the history of Millgate and its people. It is unfortunate that we have learned little more about Bridge House itself, but we have certainly learned much more about Millgate as a whole. It has proved a useful and very rewarding experience, and we are sure that Mr.Bishop, with his keen interest in the history of Aylsham, will be as pleased as the members of the History Group are about that.

THE MILLGATE DOCUMENTS

The Millgate documents, the so-called 'Bishop Bundles' which were used in the exploration of the history of Millgate and its people, belong to Tom Bishop of Bridge House. There are some 17 bundles, and a rough guide to the contents of each bundle is given below:

Bundle 1
a) Two sale notices. 1820; - 6 lots; 5 in Cromer Turnpike Rd. area.
b) Sale notice. 1845 - 3 lots, including coach and gig works.
c) Sale notice. 1830 - 4 lots, 3 of land by the river, 4th. is a cottage at Edgefield.
d) Sale notice. 1831 - 13 lots; 1 & 2 Market Place/Churchyard. 3,4,5,6 and 7 on Millgate; 8,9, & 10 (cottages -Aylsham Vicarage.) 10,11,12, & 13 on Turnpike Road.

Bundle 2
The will of James Curties 1798 and documents relating to legacies 1803-1831

Bundle 3
a) Documents relating to Thomas Cook's (Bushey) will of 1852 (?)
b) Documents relating to land, late Daniels 1906-33

Bundle 4
a) More documents relating to land as Daniels in Bundle 3.
b) Admission of Thomas Clement Francis to property, formerly of Robert Francis. 1808
c) Admission of Mrs.Anne Bircham to property formerly of Robert Francis. 1808
[This may be all the same property as bundle 3.]

Bundle 5
Documents relating to the transfer of property from Steward to Fielde on the death of John Steward. 1830

Bundle 6A

a) Copy of admission of Robert Francis. 1778
b) Conveyance of a piece of freehold land. James Mottram to
   J.B.Aldiss and others. 1901   [Aylsham Wood]
c) Copy of admission of Thomas Clement Francis. 1808
d) Copy of admission of John Fielde. 1823 [land on Ingworth Rd.]
e) Copy of admission of Mrs. & Miss Fielde. 1838
f) Copy of admission of Ann, wife of Matthias Phillippo. 1846
g) Copy of surrender by Jonas Warden and wife, to John Fielde. 1823
h) Surrender in exchange to rectify mistake - John Tuck to Ellis
   Canfer. 1817

Bundle 6B

a) Copy of admission of Sarah Parmeter (wife of Robert) to a quarter
   of the holding of Robert Francis. 1808
b) Acknowledgement of the surrender by Richard Mutten to Robert
   Parmeter. 1845
c) Search documents for 15 & 17 Millgate. 1955 & 1957.
d) Estimates for lavatories etc. and plan. 1955
e) Tithe redemption papers. 1949
f) Copy of surrender. 1869
g) Deed of enfranchisement. James Mottram 1901. [Further "Doctor's
   Pightle", "North Croft")
h) Acknowledgement of satisfaction on Richard Mutten's conditional
   surrender by Jacob Crane, 1845
i) Copy of absolute surrender by Richard Mutten and wife, to
   Mrs. Phillippo 1845.
j) Letter from solicitor to Mr.T.F.Daniels. 1920

Bundle 7

a) Abstract of title to the estate, late of James Hunt Holley,
   formerly Hawkins 1760.
b) Extract from will of George Hunt Holley - discharge for
   legacies. 1790
c) Abstract of Title of Thos.Rackham and Miss Hannah. 1757
d) Abstract of Title of Mr. John Tuck to an estate of Lancaster
   manor cottages and messuages in Millgate Street. 1831
e) Copy of admission of Ann Fielde. 1835

f) Surrender by Matthias Phillippo and Anne his wife, to the use of her will. 183?

g) Account of succession in real property, of Ann Elizabeth Aldiss, 5 Ipswich Rd. Norwich, upon the death of Matthias Phillippo.
1887

h) James Hunt Holley to Miss Ann Fielde - Act of covenant for production of title deeds. 1831

i) James Hunt Holley to Mrs John Fielde - copy of absolute surrender. 1831

j) Copy of admission - Hunt Holley to Miss Fielde. 1835

k) Copy of absolute surrender - Hunt Holley to Miss Fielde. 1831

l) Copy of admission of Mrs. Ann Eliz. Aldiss (Aylsham
Lancaster).1869

m)   "   "   " (Aylsham Wood)   1869

n) Agreement of lease for 1 year between J. B. Aldiss and I.Grimes
dated 187?

o) Footpath document - alteration, (Shepheard family?) 1896

p) Copy of admission of Ann, wife of Matthias Phillippo 1839

q) Correspondence with Mr. Phillippo about erecting a wall.

Bundle 8A

a) Document relating to the maltings as result of a dispute between Matthias Phillippo and wife, and William Belward. 1861

b) Copy of admission of Mrs. Ann Phillippo (Aylsham Wood). 1839

c) "   "   " (Aylsham Lancaster).1839

d) Surrender by Matthias Phillippo and Ann his wife to the use of her will. (Aylsham Wood) 1839

e) Copy of absolute surrender by Mr. Bartram and wife to Mrs.Phillippo (Aylsham Lancaster) 1839

f) Agreement between Matthias Phillippo and William and Robert Bartram about Doctor's Pightle. 1860

g) Receipts of quit rent from Phillippo to Parmeter. 1843

Bundle 8B

a) Copy of absolute surrender by Mr. & Miss Rackham to Mr. John Fielde. (Aylsham Wood)   1821

b) Copy of absolute surrender by Mr.R.Parmeter to Mr. J. Fielde (Aylsham Wood) 1829

c) Copy of admission of Mr.John Fielde (Aylsham Wood) 1831

d) Copy of admission of Mrs.A. Fielde, widow (Aylsham Wood) 1839
e) Copy of admission of Mr.J.Fielde (Aylsham Wood) 1822
f) Copy of absolute surrender by Mr. & Miss Rackham to
   Mr.R.Parmeter (Aylsham Wood) 1821
g) Abstract of title of Mr. & Miss Rackham to an estate - Aylsham
   ["for Mr.Fielde"] (Aylsham Wood) 1821
h) Deed of covenant for the production of deeds, Mr.T.Rackham,
   Mr.Copeman to Mr.J.Fielde. 1821
i) Copy of the will of Mr.Jonathon Custance. 1742

Bundle 9
a) Abstract of titles to copyhold estate late Ann Eliz.Aldiss.1906
b)   "   "   freehold land late Matthias Phillippo. 1906
c) Abstract of a title of Mrs. & Miss Fielde to an estate -
   Aylsham. 1778
d) Abstract of a title of Mr.Richard Mutten to an estate, Aylsham
   Copyhold of Lancaster. 1778

Bundle 10
Map of Millgate basin 1855 - named properties - Kent's Trustees,
Phillippo, Parmeter, Bane,Bircham, Wickes, Copeman, Hayne Mash.

Bundle 11
Sale documents - 1907 & 1914 - Aylsham Mill.

Bundle 12
Relates to No.46 Millgate and Maiden's Bower, inter alia, Spurrell,
Harvey, Bane, Peddar Bane.

Bundle 13
Relates to Power, Drozier and Freeman.

Bundle 14
Refers to Wood and Peterson.

Bundle 15
The Maltings.

SOURCES USED FOR THIS PROJECT

The group has drawn on a wide range of material, but the main sources were as follows:-

AYLSHAM BAPTIST Church bicentenary booklet. 1791-1991

AYLSHAM LOCAL HISTORY SOCIETY - "Journal & Newsletter" 1985 to date.
   "   "   - "Aylsham in the Seventeenth
                                         Century." 1988
   "   "   - "Aylsham in 1821" - Occasional
                                              Paper.1989

AYLSHAM Parish archives - housed in the Town Hall; in particular,
     records of the Aylsham Navigation, and of the Norwich to
     Cromer Turnpike.

BLOMEFIELD, F. An Essay towards a topographical history of
               the county of Norfolk. 2nd. ed. 11 Vols. 1810

CENSUS RETURNS: for Aylsham 1841 - 1891; in the Local Studies
                                         Library in Norwich.

CHADWICK, Owen.   Victorian Miniature. 1961

DIRECTORIES (White, Harrod, Kelly, Pigot etc.) for 19th.century

DOUGHTY, H.M. Friesland Meres and Through the Netherlands in a
               Norfolk Wherry. Jarrold & Son.

KETTON-CREMER R.W. Norfolk in the Civil War. Faber. 1969

MASON R.H. "The History of Norfolk." part 5, 1885.

MILLGATE DEEDS kindly lent by Mr.Tom Bishop

"NORFOLK ANCESTOR"

NORFOLK RECORD OFFICE [NRO] Aylsham records:
- Aylsham Tithe map: Schedule 1839. NRO 303   second copy in
  the Holley Deposit.
- Diocesan Records; wills and inventories.
- Manorial Records - Aylsham Lancaster, 17th. to 19th centuries.
              - Aylsham Vicarage , ditto
              - Aylsham Wood,   17th. and 18th centuries.
- North Walsham & Aylsham Primitive Methodist Circuit Records.
                                              NRO FC 47
- Norwich Archdeaconry Records - wills and inventories.
- Papers of Joseph Clover of Colby and of Mary Berry.
                                       NRO MC 119
- Parish [church] records   NRO PD 602
- Registers of Dissenters' Meeting Houses NRO DN/DIS/1/2

ORDNANCE SURVEY maps.

"RENTAL"   i.e. "Aylsham in the Seventeenth Century", documents
              from the Manor of Aylsham Lancaster researched by Aylsham
              Local History Society.   Poppyland Publishing. 1988

SAPWELL, John. "A history of Aylsham." 1960

WRIGHT'S map of Aylsham. 1839 and accompanying schedules.

other sources include:-

Records of births, deaths and marriages at St. Katherine's House,
London.
Wills at Somerset House, London.

----ooOoo----

INDEX